Break into English

STUDENT'S BOOK 1

Michael Carrier & Simon Haines

HODDER AND STOUGHTON

LONDON SYDNEY AUCKLAND TORONTO

Contents

1

Mark Good morning, Mrs Eastwood?
Sue Yes?
Mark I'm Mark Taylor.
Ellen And my name's Ellen.
Sue Oh yes, hello. Please come in.
. . . Excuse me.

2

Sue Hello, Colchester 84620,
Sue Eastwood here.
No, Roger isn't here.
What's your name?
Jim Baker.
Okay, goodbye.

3

Roger Hi, I'm Roger Eastwood.
Ellen Hello, I'm Ellen Taylor.
Mark And I'm Mark.
Roger What <u>do</u> you do, Ellen?
Ellen I'm a secretary.
Mark And I'm a student.
What do you do, Roger?
Roger I'm an architect.

Check! Right or wrong? (✓ or ✗)

1 My name's Sue Eastwood. ☑

2 I'm Mark Taylor. ☑

3 I'm an architect. ☑

4 My name's Ellen Taylor. I'm a secretary. ☑

Saying hello:	Hello, Good morning, Good afternoon, Good evening, Hi,	I'm	Roger Eastwood.
		My name's	Ellen Taylor.

Asking about people:	What's your name?	My name's	Mark.
		I'm	
	What do you do?	I'm	a student.
			an architect.

Numbers 1–10:

One	Two	Three	Four	Five	Six	Seven	Eight	Nine	Ten
1	2	3	4	5	6	7	8	9	10

Hello, Colchester **84620**. Sue Eastwood here.

eight four six two oh

PRACTICE

1 Read this conversation with your partner:

Mark   Hello, I'm Mark.
What's your name?
Becky   My name's Becky Goddard.
Mark   What do you do, Becky?
Becky   I'm a secretary. And you?
Mark   I'm a student.

Now you:
Make conversations like this between Chris and Ellen.

I'm a salesman.

Now you:
Talk to Roger and Becky.

2 Answer the telephone like this:

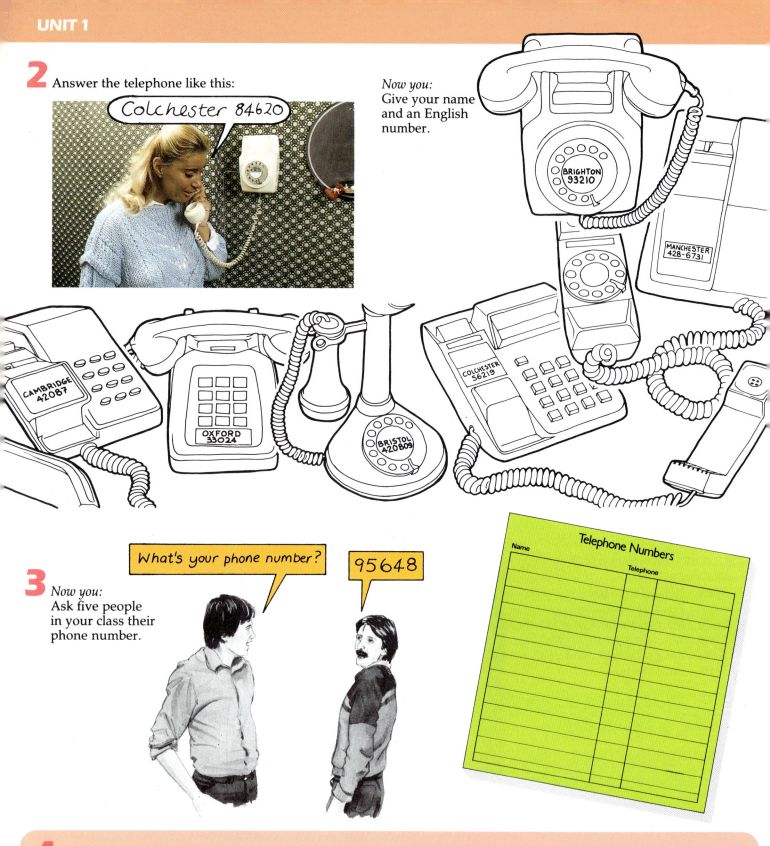

Now you:
Give your name and an English number.

Colchester 84620

BRIGHTON 93210

MANCHESTER 428-6731

CAMBRIDGE 42087

OXFORD 33024

BRISTOL 420809

COLCHESTER 56219

3 *Now you:*
Ask five people in your class their phone number.

What's your phone number?

95648

Telephone Numbers

Name		Telephone

4 **SOUNDS** Question / Answer

Listen to the cassette and repeat this question:

What's your name?

Now listen again and repeat this answer:

My name's Roger.

Now listen to the cassette and tick (✓) Question or Answer:

	1	2	3	4	5	6
Question						
Answer						

1 Make a conversation like this with your partner.

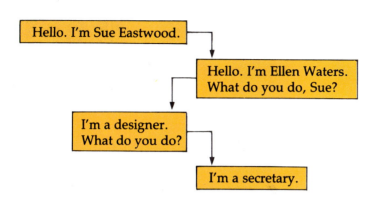

Hello. I'm Sue Eastwood.

Hello. I'm Ellen Waters. What do you do, Sue?

I'm a designer. What do you do?

I'm a secretary.

2 Now ask five people in your class.

	Name	Job
1		
2		
3		
4		
5		

3 WRITING
Fill in this form for a hotel:

GEORGE HOTEL
VISITORS REGISTER   Room No _____
Please print in CAPITAL LETTERS

Name   BRIAN BURNS
Address   6 RIVERSIDE ROAD
          CAMBRIDGE

Tel. No. (0223) 353609
Occupation ARCHITECT
Signature *Brian Burns.*

4 Now ask about two people in your class:

GEORGE HOTEL
VISITORS REGISTER   Room No _____
Please print in CAPITAL LETTERS

Name
Address

Tel. No.
Occupation
Signature

GEORGE HOTEL
VISITORS REGISTER   Room No _____
Please print in CAPITAL LETTERS

Name
Address

Tel. No.
Occupation
Signature

Language Summary

Now you know how to:

- **Say hello:**
  Hi.
  Good morning.

- **Introduce yourself:**
  I'm Mark Waters.
  My name's Ellen.

- **Ask about people:**
  What's your name?   *My name's Roger Eastwood.*
  What do you do?   *I'm a student.*
  What's your address?   *7 Royal Terrace, Colchester.*

- **Use the numbers one to ten.**

1

Sarah   Hello.
Sue   Oh, hello. This is Sarah.
Sarah, this is Ellen and Mark.
Sarah   Pleased to meet you.
Ellen   Hello.
Mark   Pleased to meet you.

2

Sarah   What do you do, Ellen?
Ellen   I'm a secretary.
Mark   What do you do, Chris?
Chris   I'm a salesman.
Sarah   Where are you from?
Ellen   We're from Los Angeles.

3

Roger   Hello, Ellen. How are you?
Ellen   I'm fine thanks. And you?
Roger   I'm okay.

Check!   Right or wrong? (✓ or ✗)

3   We're from America. ☑

4   I'm a salesman. ☑

1   I'm Sue. ☐

2   I'm a secretary. ☑

Introducing people:	Sarah, this is Ellen and Mark.	Pleased to meet you.
	This is Chris.	

Saying hello:	How are you?	I'm fine,	thanks.	And you?
		I'm okay,		How are you?

Asking for information:	Where are you from?	I'm	from	Colchester.
		We're		the United States.

Numbers 11–20: ■■■■■■■■

PRACTICE

1 Introduce these people to your partner.

Now you:
Introduce two people in your class to your partner.

How are you?

I'm fine, thanks.

2 *Now you:*
Talk to your partner.

3 Finish this conversation with your partner.

Mark   Hello, I'm ~~mark~~ What's your ~~name~~?
Sarah ~~my~~ name's ~~Sarah~~.
Mark   ~~what do you~~ do?
Sarah ~~I'm such~~ reporter. What ~~do you do~~?
Mark   I'm ~~a~~ student.
Sarah ~~where are you~~ from?
Mark   ~~I'm from~~ Los Angeles.

4 You are one of these people. Make a conversation with your partner.

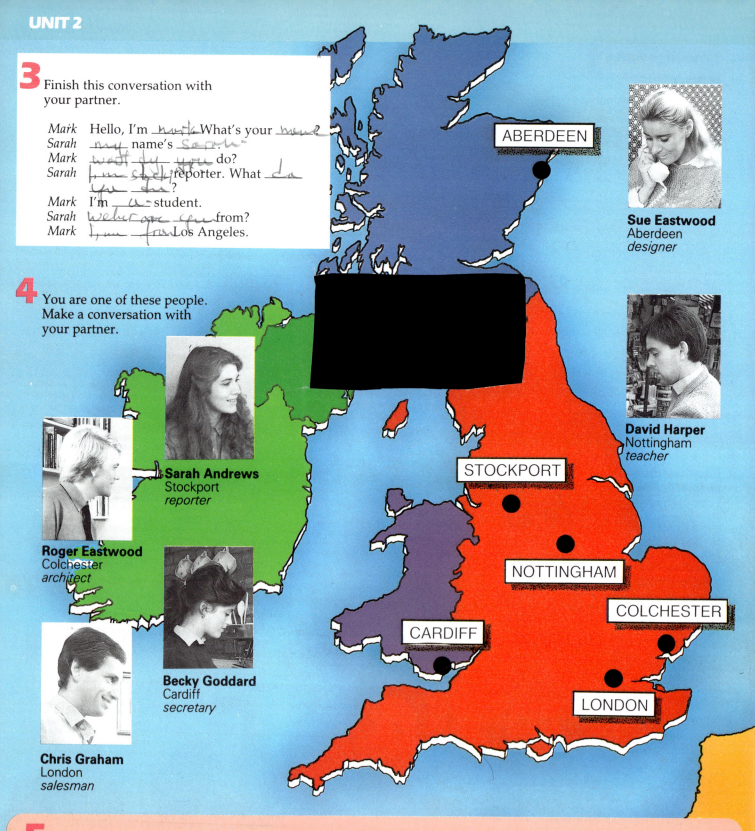

Sue Eastwood
Aberdeen
designer

David Harper
Nottingham
teacher

Sarah Andrews
Stockport
reporter

Roger Eastwood
Colchester
architect

Becky Goddard
Cardiff
secretary

Chris Graham
London
salesman

ABERDEEN
STOCKPORT
NOTTINGHAM
CARDIFF
COLCHESTER
LONDON

5 SOUNDS   Question / Answer

Listen to the cassette and repeat this question:

   What do you do?

Now listen again and repeat this answer:

   I'm a salesman.

Now listen to the cassette and tick (✓) Question or Answer:

	1	2	3	4	5	6
Question						
Answer						

TRANSFER

1 Fill in the missing words:

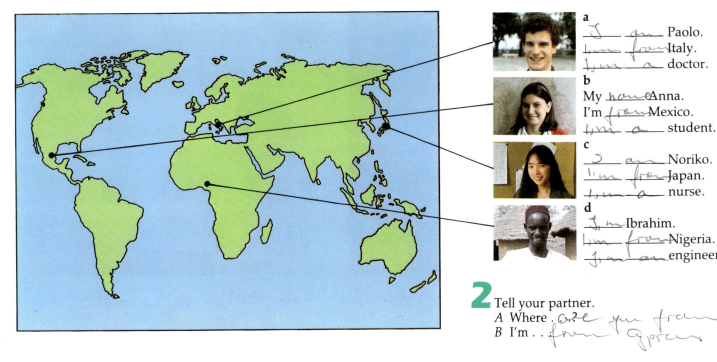

a
I am Paolo.
I'm from Italy.
I'm a doctor.

b
My name Anna.
I'm from Mexico.
I'm a student.

c
I am Noriko.
I'm from Japan.
I'm a nurse.

d
I'm Ibrahim.
I'm from Nigeria.
I'm an engineer.

2 Tell your partner.
A Where are you from?
B I'm from Greece.

3 WRITING
Write a notice
for yourself.

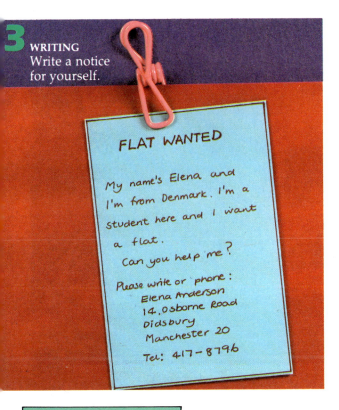

FLAT WANTED

My name's Elena and
I'm from Denmark. I'm a
student here and I want
a flat.
Can you help me?

Please write or phone:
Elena Anderson
14, Osborne Road
Didsbury
Manchester 20
Tel: 417-8796

4 GAME

1 Good _____ . How are you?
2 What do you do, Mark? I'm a _____ .
3 What do you do, Ellen? I'm a _____ .
4 Hello _____ 84620.
5 What's _____ name?
6 Where are you from, Paolo? I'm from _____ .

5 LISTENING Write about the four people.

	1	2	3	4
name:	Ian Edwards			
from:			Barcelona	
job:		doctor		

Language Summary

Now you know how to:

- **Ask for information:**
  Where are you from? *I'm from Spain.*
  We're from the United States.

- **Use the numbers eleven to twenty**

- **Say hello:**
  How are you? *I'm fine thanks.*

- **Introduce people:**
  This is Ellen. *Pleased to meet you.*

1

Mark   Morning Roger. Are you busy?
Roger No, I'm not. Come in.

2

Ellen Who's that?
Roger It's Rachel.
Ellen Is she at home?
Roger No, she isn't.
         She's at school today.

3

Mark   Who's that with Becky?
Roger It's David.
Mark   What does he do?
Roger He's a teacher.
Mark   Where's he from?
Roger Nottingham, I think.

4

David Who are the people with Roger?
Becky Ellen and Mark. They're in Flat 3.
David Where are they from?
Becky They're from the United States.

Check! Right or wrong? (✓ or ✗)
1 Rachel is at home today. ✗
2 David is from London. ✗
3 Mark and Ellen are from the United States. ✓

Asking about people:

Who's that?	It's	David.
		Roger and Sue.

Is	he / she	from Liverpool?	Yes, / No,	he is. / she isn't.

Are	they / Mark and Ellen	from the United States?	Yes, / No,	they	are. / aren't.

Are you busy?	Yes, I am.
	No, I'm not.

The verb BE:

Short form	Long form
I'm	I am
you're	you are
she's	she is
he's	he is
it's	it is
we're	we are
they're	they are

Talking about jobs:

What does	Sarah / Roger	do?	She's an architect. / He's a reporter.

What do	they / Mark and John	do?	They / Mark and John	are students.

Talking about places:

Where's	Rachel?	She's	at	home. / school.

PRACTICE

1 Ask your partner about these people.

A Where's . . .? Is she / he at . . .?

B Yes / No . . . She's / He's . . .

RACHEL

MICHAEL AND PENNY

JUNE

PETER, JOHN AND ANDREW

SALLY

PHILIP

2 Talk to your partner about these people.

A Who's that?
B That's Mr Silver.
A What does he do?
B He's an engineer.
A Where's he from?
B He's from Cardiff, in Wales.

Mrs Hall
secretary
Colchester

Mr Hall
salesman
Colchester

Mr Silver
engineer
Cardiff

Mr and Mrs Francis
architect   teacher
Glasgow   Glasgow

Mrs Perry
designer
Bristol

3 Ask your partner about these cars.

A Is it a Volvo?
B Yes . . .
   No . . .   It's . . .

VOLVO

RENAULT

FIAT

V·A·G Audi VW

---

4 SOUNDS   Long / Short

🔊 Listen to the cassette and repeat these **long** forms:

    I am / is not / there is

Now listen again and repeat these **short** forms:

    I'm / isn't / there's

Now listen to the cassette and tick (✓) long or short:

	1	2	3	4	5	6
Long						
Short						

TRANSFER

1 GROUPWORK

Write your telephone number, your job and where you are from, on a piece of paper. Put all the pieces of paper in a box. Now take one piece of paper and find the person. Ask questions like these:

Are you from . . . ?
Is your telephone number . . . ?

2 READING

Look at these people on holiday. Stanley's an engineer, from Leeds. He's next to Carol, a teacher from Glasgow. Alan's from Brighton. He's a student at university. Jim and Jo are from Luton. He's a doctor, and she's a teacher at Luton School.

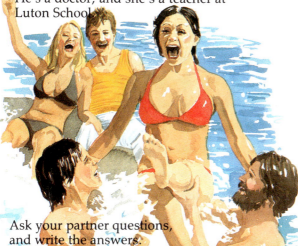

Ask your partner questions, and write the answers.

Question	Answer
Jim / Luton?	
Carol / secretary?	
Stanley / architect?	
Jo / Liverpool?	
Alan / student?	
Carol / Aberdeen?	
Jo / doctor?	
Jim / teacher?	

3 GAME

Who are these people? Use the information below to fill in the tables.

Melina	rockstar	United States
Jane	Bowie	politician
Greece	David	Hoffman
Australia	Richards	Dustin
writer	filmstar	Mercouri	Britain

Name?
Job?
From?

Name?
Job?
From?

Name?
Job?
From?

Name?
Job?
From?

4

 Talk to your partner about these people.
- Who's that?
- Where's she/he from?
- What does she/he do?
- Is she/he a . . . ?

Language Summary

Now you know how to:

- **Ask about people and give short answers:**
  Are you from Bristol?   *Yes, I am.*
  Is she at home?   *No, she isn't.*
  Are they tourists?   *No, they aren't.*
  Where's he from?   *Liverpool.*

- **Ask WHO questions:**
  Who's that?   *It's Sarah.*

- **Ask about jobs:**
  What does he do?   *He's an architect.*

- **Talk about places:**
  Where's Roger?   *He's at home.*

1

Ellen This is Roger's flat, and that's Sarah and Becky's, downstairs.
That's Chris and David's flat, and this is our flat. Come in.

Jane Oh, it's really lovely.

2

Mark This is the bathroom, and the kitchen here has a washing machine, a fridge, a cooker and a freezer. *bacydolub / donduron Sep-*

Jane What's in here?

Ellen It's the living room.

Jane It's great, but where's the television?

Ellen Oh, it's in the bedroom.

Jane What's this?

Mark Oh, it's just a cupboard.

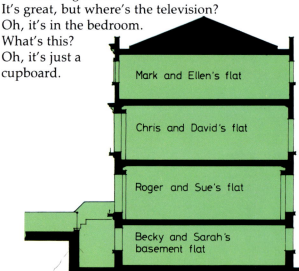

Mark and Ellen's flat

Chris and David's flat

Roger and Sue's flat

Becky and Sarah's basement flat

Check! Right or wrong? (✓ or ✗)

1 Mark and Ellen's kitchen has a fridge and a freezer. ☑
2 Sarah's flat is downstairs. ☑
3 The television is in the kitchen. ☒

Language Focus

Describing places:

This is Roger's flat.		
That's the kitchen.		

The living room	has a	television.
It		sofa.

Asking about things and places:

What's	this?	It's	the fridge.
	that?		a cupboard.

Where's the	television?	It's in the	bedroom.
	fridge?		kitchen.

Possessives:

This is	Roger's	flat.
	Chris and David's	

The verb HAVE:

I you we they	have	he she it	has

1 Ask your partner about the things in the picture, using the words in the box.
    What's this?
    It's a . . .

a spoon
a knife
a fork
a teaspoon
a bowl
a plate
a cup
a saucer

2 Talk about these rooms with your partner.
    This is _____'s room.
    It has . . .

Sally's room

Nick's room

3 GAME
Look at the two rooms for ten seconds, and then close the book.

Now you:
Ask your partner questions like this:
A   Where's the fridge?
B   It's in _____'s room.

4 Look at this map and ask your partner:

Where's the . . . ?
It's in _____ Street.

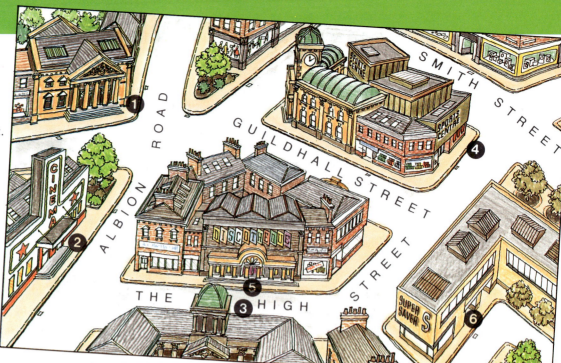

KEY

1 theatre
2 cinema
3 museum
4 sports centre
5 discotheque
6 supermarket

5 **SOUNDS**   Chris /ɪ/~ please /i:/

Listen to the cassette and repeat these words with /ɪ/:

Chris / think / with

Listen again and repeat these words with /i:/:

me / please / meet

Now listen to the cassette and tick /ɪ/ or /i:/

	1	2	3	4	5	6
/ɪ/						
/i:/						

TRANSFER

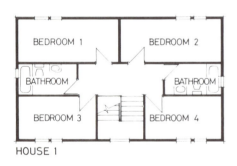

HOUSE 1

HOUSE 2

HOUSE 3

HOUSE 4

1 **LISTENING**
Listen to the cassette and write the numbers of the houses.

Mr Smith's house _____   Jane Ferry's house _____

Mrs Brown's house _____   Mr and Mrs Harris's house _____

2 Draw a plan of your house or flat or office and give it to your partner. Answer your partners questions about it.

3 Now write on your plan, like this:

THIS IS THE ....

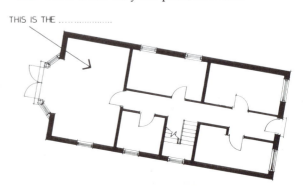

4 Ask your partner about this car, using the words in the box.
What's . . .?

the engine

a seat

the roof

a headlight

a window

a door

a wheel

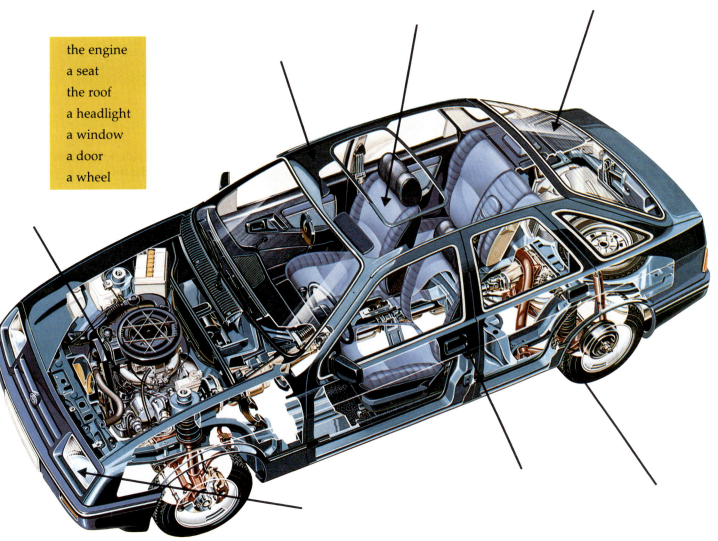

5 GROUPWORK
Draw a map of the centre of your town or village.
Give it to your partners.
Ask them about the places in your town.
Where's the . . .?

6 WORDS
Find 4 rooms and 4 things in rooms.
Then make sentences like this:
LALH/BLATE — HALL/TABLE
The table is in the hall.

ROODBEM   ROOCEK   NICKHET   HAIRC

EELVIISONT   THBA   VIIRMGNOOL   BATMOHOR

Language Summary

Now you know how to:

- **Ask about things and places:**
  What's this?   *It's a cup.*
  What's that?   *It's the bathroom.*
  Where's the television?   *It's in the bedroom.*

- **Describe places:**
  The dining room has a table and four chairs.
  This is the living room.
  That's the bathroom.

- **Say who owns things:**
  This is David's flat.
  That's John's car.

- **Use the verb HAVE**

1

Roger Here's a guide to Colchester, with a map of the town.
Mark Thanks. Where's Royal Terrace?
Roger It's here. And here's the town centre.
Mark Is this the shopping centre?
Roger No, it isn't. That's the bus station. This is the shopping centre, here.
Mark Is there a sports centre?
Roger Yes there is. It's here, in the park.
Mark And where's the station?
Roger Well, there are two stations. One for trains to London, and one for trains to Clacton. This is the station for London.

2

Ellen Excuse me, is this the train for London?
Guard Yes, it is.
Ellen When does it leave?
Guard It leaves at ten o'clock.
Ellen And when does it arrive in London?
Guard At eleven.
Ellen Thank you.

Check! Right or wrong? (✓ or ✗)

1 There are two stations in Colchester. ☐
2 The London train leaves at eleven o'clock. ☐
3 There is a sports centre in the park. ☐

Asking for information about places:

| Is this | the shopping centre? | Yes, it is. |
| | the station? | No, it isn't. |

Talking about times:

| When does | it | leave? | It | leaves at 10 o'clock. |
| | the train | arrive? | | arrives at 11 o'clock. |

Describing places:

| There's a theatre | in the town. |
| There are two stations | |

| Is there | a sports centre? | Yes, there is. |
| | an airport? | No, there isn't. |

PRACTICE

1 Ask your partner about this attic.

A   Is there a . . .?

B   Yes, there is.
Yes, there's a . . .

2 Ask your partner.
- When does the . . . open?
- When does it close?

SUPERMARKET

BOOKSHOP

TRAVEL AGENT

CAFÉ

JOB CENTRE

GREENGROCER

18

3 Ask your partner about the pictures.

A Is this a . . . ?

B Yes
No . . .

bridge
church
mosque
factory
castle
power-station

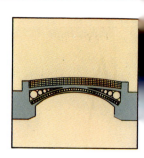

4 SOUNDS   bid /ɪ/ ~ bed /e/

Listen to the cassette and repeat these words with /ɪ/:

in / Chris / this

Listen again and repeat these words with /e/:

bed / Ben / red

Now listen to the cassette and tick /ɪ/ or /e/:

	1	2	3 .	4	5	6	7	8
/ɪ/								
/e/								

TRANSFER

1 Spot the difference. Talk about these pictures and find nine differences between the two pictures.

Is there a . . . in picture 1?

1

2

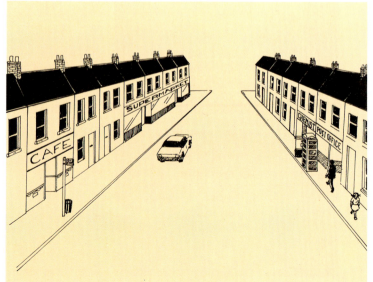

2 Read this conversation

Is there a disco in Colchester?

Yes, there is. It's in Church Street.

Oh good. When does it open?

It opens at nine o'clock, I think.

Now talk to your partners about these things in your town:

– a disco
– a sports club
– a supermarket
– a museum
– a theatre
– a restaurant

3 LISTENING
Listen to the train times at Colchester Station. Write the times and platform numbers.

Platform Number	Train to	Leaves at	Arrives at
4	London		
	Clacton		
	Norwich	3·00	
	London		

4 WRITING
An American friend wants to visit your town.
Write about the things in your town, like this:

Dear Rick,

There's a cinema and a good local museu... but there isn't a thea... There is a swimmi... and there are ten... courts and a sq...

Yours
Bruce

1-64-02-09

A SALMON CAMERACOLOUR POST CARD

Language Summary

Now you know how to:

● **Ask for information about places:**
  Is this the station? *Yes, it is.*
  Is there a station? *Yes, there are two stations.*

● **Ask about times:**
  When does it open? *It opens at nine o'clock.*

● **Describe places:**
  There's a disco in Church Street.
  There are three chairs in the attic.
  There isn't a museum.

20

UNIT 6 Jobs and interests

1

Ellen So John is your cousin, Becky?

Becky That's right. He comes to Colchester at the weekend.

Ellen Where does he live?

Becky He lives in Chelmsford, but his family comes from Birmingham.

Ellen What does he do?

Becky He's a manager, I think. He works for Marconi in Chelmsford.

Ellen Why does he come to Colchester?

Becky Well, he goes to the football . . . and he likes Sarah, too, of course.

2

John So, what do you and Ellen do in the evening in Colchester?

Mark Oh, different things. There's a lot to do here, you know. We go to the theatre or the university film club. Ellen and her friends go to the sports centre. They love tennis. I play football, and we go to the pub, of course.

John Where do you play football?

Mark At the university. I play for the student team.

Check! Right or wrong? (✓ or ✗)

1 John lives in Colchester. ☒
2 Sarah is John's cousin. ☒
3 Mark plays football for the student team. ☒
4 Mark and Ellen go to Chelmsford at the weekend. ☐

Language Focus

Asking about people:

| Where | do | you they | live? | I We They | live | in London. |
| | does | he she | | He She | lives | |

| What | do | you they | do at the the weekend? | I We They | go | to the theatre. |
| | does | she he | | She He | goes | |

| Why | do | you they | come to Colchester? | I We They | work | here. |
| | does | he she | | He She | works | |

Times:

| I play tennis **in the evening**. | We go to the cinema **at the weekend**. |
| He goes to work **in the morning**. | The shop opens **at 9 o'clock** . |

SARAH	BECKY	ELLEN	MARK
Flat 1	Flat 1	Flat 3	Flat 3
Colchester	Colchester	London	Colchester
reporter	secretary	secretary	student
go to the cinema	go to the theatre	listen to music	watch TV
go ice-skating	play tennis	play squash	play football

1 Finish this conversation with your partner.

Now you:
Make more conversations like this with Becky, Ellen and Mark.

A	Where do you live, Sarah?
Sarah	. . .
A	Where do you work?
Sarah	. . .
A	What do you do?
Sarah	. . .
A	What do you do in the evening?
Sarah	. . .
A	What do you do at the weekend?
Sarah	. . .

2 Talk to your partner about Ben and Hannah.
- Where does he . . .?
- What does she . . .?
- Where do they . . .?

Ben

ADDRESS: 19, Drury Road

JOB: Engineer

PLACE OF WORK: London

HOBBIES: Theatre and Squash

Hannah

ADDRESS: 17, Halifax Road

JOB: Social worker

PLACE OF WORK: London

HOBBIES: Tennis and Music

3 Ask your partner about
the woman in the pictures.

A When does Jane . . . ?

B She . . . | at . . .
         | in . . .

4 SOUNDS   Yes /s/ ~ has /z/

Listen to the cassette and repeat these
words with /s/:

    Yes / course / Sue

Now listen again and repeat these words
with /z/:

    does / busy / has

Now listen to the cassette and tick /s/ or /z/:

	1	2	3	4	5	6	7	8
/s/								
/z/								

TRANSFER

1 GROUPWORK
Interview four
people in your
class and fill in
the questionnaire.

2 PAIRWORK
Talk to your
partner about the
other people.

	Student 1	Student 2	Student 3	Student 4
name				
address				
from				
free time				
evenings and weekends				
place of work or study				

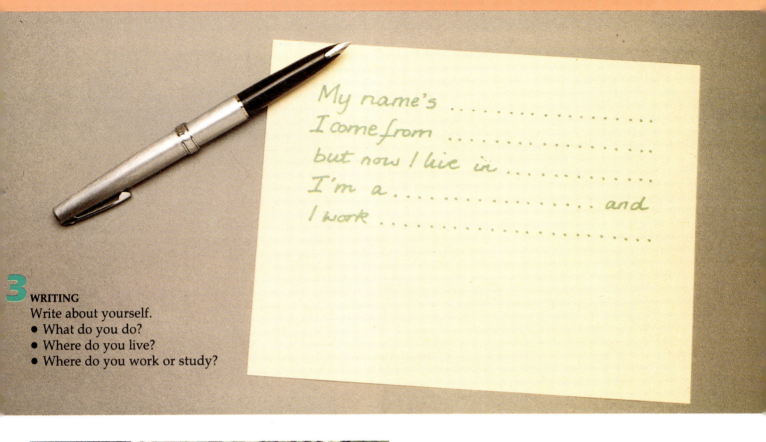

On the note (handwritten):

My name's ....
I come from ....
but now I live in ....
I'm a .... and
I work ....

3 WRITING

Write about yourself.
- What do you do?
- Where do you live?
- Where do you work or study?

4 READING

Paul is a lawyer in London:

I live in north London but I come from Manchester. My parents still live there, with my two sisters. I work in central London, for a big international company. My job is international law. I write the international contracts for the company. It's a good job.

Finish these sentences about Paul.
1 Paul _works_ in central London.
2 He comes from _Manchester_
3 He is a _lawyer_
4 He writes _____ for the company.
international contracts

5 LISTENING

Listen to Ken. Write down what he does, where he lives, and where he comes from.

Language Summary

Now you know how to:

- **Ask and give information about people:**
  Where does he work?   *He works in London.*
  What do they do at the weekend?   *They go to the cinema.*
  Why do you come to Colchester?   *I work here.*

- **Talk about times:**
  He goes to work in the morning.
  It opens at 9 o'clock.

1

Interviewer	Excuse me, I work for the BBC. Can I ask you about the television programmes you watch?
Woman	Yes, of course.
Interviewer	Do you live in Colchester?
Woman	Yes, I do.
Interviewer	How old are you?
Woman	I'm twenty-five.
Interviewer	Do you watch TV at the weekend?
Woman	Yes.
Interviewer	Do you watch the late film on Friday?
Woman	No, I don't.
Interviewer	Do you like comedy programmes?
Woman	Yes, I do. I love comedy.
Interviewer	Do you watch the nine o'clock news on Saturday and Sunday?
Woman	Yes. Always.
Interviewer	And do you . . .

2

Interviewer	Do you like sports programmes?
Man	Yes, I do, especially the football.
Interviewer	Does your wife watch the football with you?
Man	No, she doesn't. She hates sport.
Interviewer	Now, your children. Do they watch TV on Saturday?
Man	Yes, they do. They watch children's television in the morning.
Interviewer	Do they watch in the evening?
Man	No, they don't. They go to bed at eight o'clock.
Interviewer	That's all. Thank you for your help.
Man	That's okay.

Check! Right or wrong? (✓ or ✗)
1 The woman is 35. ✗
2 She likes comedy programmes. ✓
3 She lives in Colchester. ✓

Check! Right or wrong? (✓ or ✗)
1 The man doesn't watch football. ✗
2 His wife doesn't like football. ✓
3 The children watch TV in the evening. ✗

Asking questions:

Do	you / they / your children	watch TV?	Yes / No	I / we / they	do. / don't.

Does	she / your wife	like football?	Yes / No	she	does. / doesn't.

Age and numbers:

HOW OLD ARE YOU?

I'M THIRTY TWO.

Days of the week:

PRACTICE

1 Ask the people in the photographs questions like this:

You   Do you watch the news?
Sue   Yes, I do.
You   Do you and Roger like sport?
Sue   No, we don't.

PROGRAMMES	Sue and Roger		Sarah	Chris
The News	✓	✓	✓	✓
Comedy programmes	✗	✓	✓	✗
Films	✓	✗	✓	✗
Sports programmes	✗	✗	✓	✓
Documentaries	✓	✓	✗	✓
Cartoons	✗	✗	✗	✗

2 Ask about the people in the photographs.

A   Does Sarah like documentaries?
B   No, she doesn't.
A   Do Sue and Roger watch the news?
B   Yes, they do.

3 Fill in this chart and add more questions.

What do you do on . . .?	Monday	Tuesday	Wednesday	Thursday	Friday	Saturday	Sunday
Watch TV							
Play sport							
Read							

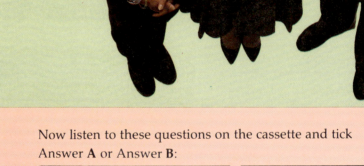

4 Ask about these people
A   How old is . . .?
B   He's fifty-two.

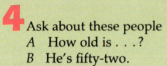

1	52
2	26
3	24
4	29
5	38
6	58

Now you:
Write the names of four people –
friends or family – and show them to
your partner.

Make conversations like this:
A   How old is . . .?
B   He's . . .

5 SOUNDS   Questions and answers

Listen to the cassette and repeat this
question and answer:

Is he from London?   Yes, he is.

Now listen to the cassette again and
repeat this question and answer:

Who's that?   It's David.

Now listen to these questions on the cassette and tick
Answer **A** or Answer **B**:

1	**A** Yes, it's Sue.	
	B My name's Sue.	
2	**A** No, I'm not.	
	B I'm a doctor.	
3	**A** Yes, I do.	
	B We live in Colchester.	

4	**A** No, I don't.	
	B I work in London.	
5	**A** Yes, I am.	
	B I'm from Manchester.	
6	**A** No, he doesn't.	
	B He doesn't like football.	

TRANSFER

1 GROUPWORK

Find out about your partners.
Ask questions like this:

- Do you like hamburgers?
- Do you eat . . .?
- Do you drink . . .?

Food and Drink survey

	Partner 1		
Name			
Age			
Food: hamburgers			
pizza			
ice-cream			
. . .			
. . .			
Drink: coffee			
tea			
wine			
. . .			
. . .			

2 WRITING

RESULTS OF THE TV SURVEY IN COLCHESTER

Write a report of your group's Food and Drink survey, like the one above.
75% of the group eat hamburgers, but only 25% like pizza . . .

3 GAME

Think of a number between 10 and 99. (47)
Add the two numbers together (4 + 7 = 11).
Tell your partner the answer (11).
Your partner now tries to find the first number (47).

A Is it 38?
B No, it isn't.

A Is it 65?
B No, it isn't.

A Is it 47?
B Yes, it is.

4 LISTENING

Listen to the cassette and write the population of the countries on this chart.

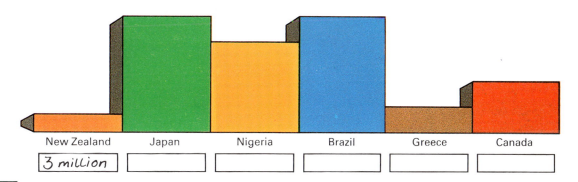

New Zealand	Japan	Nigeria	Brazil	Greece	Canada
3 million					

Language Summary

Now you know how to:

- **Ask questions and give short answers:**

  Do you watch the news? *Yes, I do.*
  No, I don't.

  Does he like football? *Yes, he does.*
  No, he doesn't.

- **Talk about ages:**

  How old are you? *I'm thirty-two.*

- **Talk about days of the week:**

  We watch the late film on Friday.

A day in the life of . . .

Sita Williams works at Gatwick Airport, in London. She works at the information desk. She gives people information about the arrivals and departures of planes.

🔊 LISTENING

Sita is talking about her job and what she does in her day. Write in the missing information.

SITA'S DAY	
time	*action*
5 am	get up
	start work
	have lunch

A day in the life of . . .

Paul Martin works at the airport as an air traffic controller. He works for eight hours a day, from 8 am to 4 pm or from 4 pm to midnight. He likes his job, because he works with planes and pilots – not with passengers. 'It's not easy to work with passengers', he says.

Paul's job is not easy. Gatwick is a very busy place. Every year 28 million passengers use Gatwick Airport, and every day 900 to a 1000 planes take off or land.

Check!

1 What does Paul do?
2 How many planes land or take off every day?
3 Does Paul like his job?
4 When does Paul work?
5 How many passengers use Gatwick every year?

WRITING

Write about a different job.
– a postman
– a doctor
– an air stewardess
– a taxi driver

What does he or she do every day?

First floor plan of Terminal 1

	Departure lounge		Bar
Restaurant			
	Duty free shop	Duty free shop	
Restaurant	Gift shop	Passport Control	Computer shop	Bookshop	Bar
				Information desk	
Book shop		C h e c k - i n d e s k s			
		1 2 3 4 5 6 7 8			

What is there in the terminal?

There's a . . .
There are two . .

1

Chris Hi Andy. Is this your new car?
Andy Yes, it is. Do you like it?
Chris It's beautiful. Is it fast?
Andy Yes, of course it is. It's very fast. It's got a two litre engine, electric windows and an expensive stereo.
Chris It's very nice.
Andy What <u>sort</u> of car have you got?
Chris I've got an old Mini, but I really want a new car. My car's okay, but it hasn't got a stereo or electric windows. And it's very slow.

2

Sue Right, we've got our shopping. Now, where's the car?
Roger It's here. Hey, there's Andy in his new car.

Check! Right or wrong? (✓ or ✗)
1 Chris has got a new car. ☒
2 Andy's car is very fast. ☑
3 Chris's car has got a stereo and electric windows. ☒
4 Chris wants a new car. ☑
5 Chris likes Andy's car. ☐

Talking about possessions:

I've You've We've They've She's He's	got an old Renault but	I you we they	want	a new car.
		she he	wants	

I You We They	haven't	got a big car.	Have you	got a fast car?	Yes, I have.
He She	hasn't		Has she		No, she hasn't.

Saying who owns things:

It's	my your his her our their	room.

Adjectives:

Andy's car is very	new. fast. big. expensive.

It isn't	an	old	car.
	a	slow small cheap	

1 A What sort of car has he got?
B He's got an old Citroen, but he wants a Volkswagen.

Now ask questions about the people in the pictures.

Mini

Vauxhall

Citroen

Mercedes

Volkswagen

Volvo

2 Ask your partner questions like this:

A   Have you got a fast car?
B   No, I haven't.   I've got a slow car.
                     My car's very slow.

fast	slow	cheap	expensive
old	new	big	small

3 Ask about David and his family
A   Who's that?
B   It's his mother. David's her son.

BRIAN = BRENDA

4 Now write your family tree.
Talk to your partner about
the people in your family,
and ask about his or her
family.
A   This is Peter. He's my
     brother.
     This is . . .

ALISON   DAVID   PETER   CAROLINE

5 SOUNDS   day /d/ ~ table /t/

🔊 Listen to the cassette and repeat these
words with /d/:

day / London / bed

Listen again and repeat these words with
/t/:

table / Italy / not

Now listen to the cassette and tick /d/ or /t/:

	1	2	3	4	5	6	7	8
/d/								
/t/								

TRANSFER

1 Ask your partner about his or her
possessions.
Ask questions like this about the things
in the picture:

● Have you got a TV?
● What sort of . . . have you got?
● Has it got a . . .?
● Do you want a . . .?

2

STUDENT A

Ask your partner about his or her car:

- Sort of car?
- New?
- Good?
- Like it?
- 4 doors or 2 doors?
- Stereo?
- Comfortable?
- Fast?

STUDENT B

Answer your partner's questions about your car:

- Mini.
- 10 years old.
- 2 doors.
- Uncomfortable.
- No stereo.
- Slow, but you like it.

3 **LISTENING** Listen to the cassette, and write in the information about the hotels.

	Hotel Bristol	Hotel Fantastic
number of rooms?		
swimming pool?		
bar?		
discotheque?		
number of stars?		
price per night?		
old or new?		
big or small?		

4 **WRITING**
You have a:
– new house
– new car
– new camera
Describe it.

My new _____ is very _____. It's got _____ and _____

Language Summary

Now you know how to:

- **Talk about possessions:**
  I've got a new flat.
  He hasn't got a car.

- **Say who owns things:**
  It's his camera.
  That's my hat.

- **Describe things:**
  It's big and very expensive.

34

Woman	Excuse me. Can you tell me where the George Hotel is, please?
Roger	Certainly. We're in Nunns Road. Turn right at the end of this road.
Woman	Turn right. Yes.
Roger	Then turn left at the end of East Stockwell Street into the High Street. The George is on the left, opposite Woolworths.
Woman	Can I park there?
Roger	Yes, there's a car park behind the hotel, I think.
Woman	Thanks very much.

How to find us:

★ Leave the bypass at the roundabout.
★ Go straight on at the first traffic lights.
★ Drive up North Hill.
★ Turn left at the traffic lights.
★ Go along the High Street.
★ The George is on the left between East Stockwell Street and Maidenburgh Street.

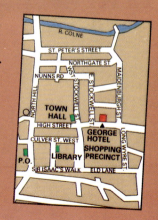

Check! Answer these questions **Yes, it is** or **No, it isn't.**

1 Is the George Hotel in Nunns Road? *No, it isn't*
2 Is the hotel behind Woolworths? *No, it isn't.*
3 Is the car park behind the hotel? *Yes, it is*
4 Is the hotel between East Stockwell Street and West Stockwell Street? *No, it isn't*

Asking for directions:	Can you tell me where the George Hotel is, please?	
	Where's Where is	the George Hotel, please?

Giving directions:	Turn	right left	at the traffic lights.	Go straight on.

	Go along	the High Street. this road.

Saying where things or places are:	The car park is	behind the hotel. between East Stockwell Street and Maidenburgh Street.
	The George Hotel is	in the High Street. on the left. opposite Woolworths.

PRACTICE

1 Ask for directions like this:

A   Can you tell me where Flat 3 is, please?
B   Yes, go along the corridor, turn left,
    and it's on your left.

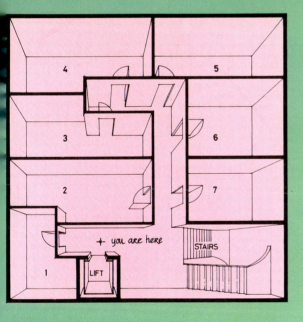

2 Now ask your partner like this:

A   Where's the newsagent?
B   It's next to the Post Office.
A   What's behind the church?
B   The pub.

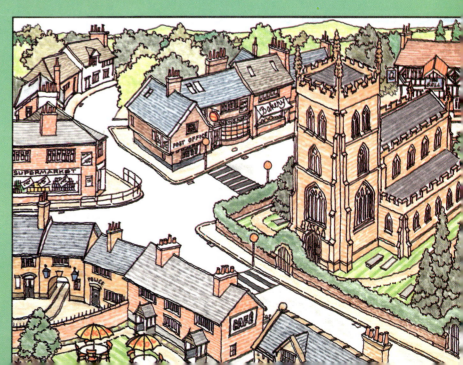

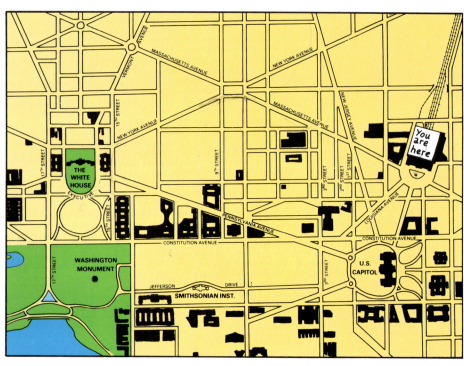

3 Look at the map and fill in the missing words.

A Excuse me. Can you tell me where the White House is, please?

B Yes, certainly. We're in the station. Now, _turn a long_ into Massachusetts Avenue. Go _right_ on. Then turn _left_ into New York Avenue.

A _Turn_ left, okay.

B Go _straight_. Then turn _left_ into Executive Avenue.

A And then?

B The White House is on the _right_.

Now make more conversations with your part~

You are at:
– The White House
– The Washington Monument
– The station

Give directions to:
– The Capitol
– The station
– The Smithsonian Institute

---

4 SOUNDS   park /p/ ~ book /b/

Listen to the cassette and repeat these words with /p/:

park / computer / help

Listen again and repeat these words with /b/:

book / football / club

Now listen to the cassette and tick /p/ or /b/:

	1	2	3	4	5	6	7	8
/p/								
/b/								

TRANSFER

1 Ask your partner for directions. Start like this:

Excuse me. Can you tell me where Mill Road is, please?

You are
  on the road from Basingford
You want
  the Barrats' house

You are
  in Bridge Street
You want
  the Simpsons' house

You are
  at the Simpsons' house
You want
  the road to Sevenbridge

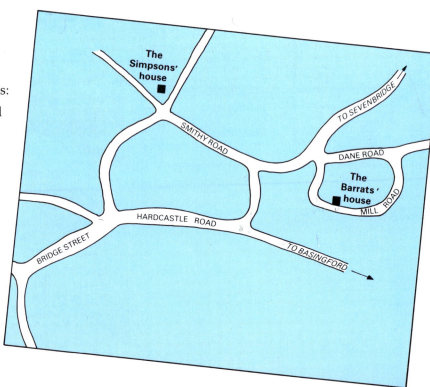

WRITING

Write directions from
your home to:
– the town centre.
– the cinema.
– the railway station.
– your school, college
    or office.

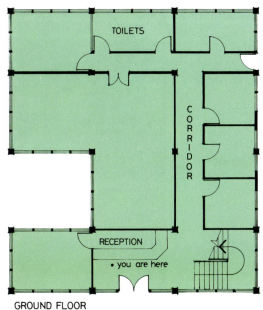

LISTENING

Listen to the cassette and find
these places on the plan:
– Mr Johnson's room
– the canteen
– Miss Richard's office
– Mrs Nelson's room

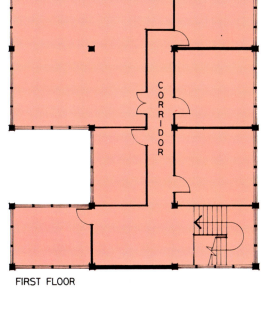

FIRST FLOOR

TOILETS

CORRIDOR

RECEPTION

• you are here

GROUND FLOOR

GAME
Your partner wants to
go from B to A.
Give directions.

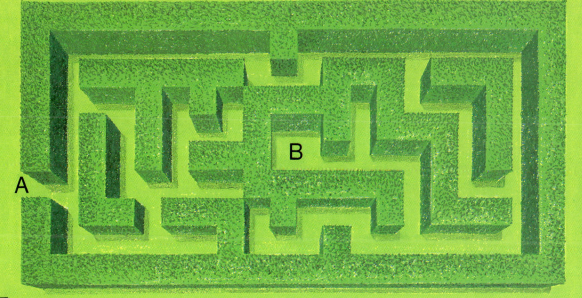

A

B

Language Summary

*Now you
know
how to:*

● **Ask for directions:**
    Can you tell me where the George Hotel is, please?

● **Give directions:**
    Turn left and go along the High Street.

● **Say where things and places are:**
    It's on the left.
    It's behind the hotel.
    It's opposite Woolworths.

1

Travel agent	Good morning. Can I help you?
Husband	Good morning. I'd like some information about planes to Mexico City, please.
Travel agent	Mexico City. Certainly. When would you like to fly?
Husband	Are there any planes on Sunday?
Travel agent	Yes, there are two. One at a quarter past ten in the morning and one at a quarter to nine in the evening.
Husband	I think we'd like to take the eight forty-five flight.
Travel agent	That's flight BA 1998. Can you give me your phone number, please?
Husband	It's 987-2314. Can you phone us tomorrow with the ticket information?
Travel agent	Yes, of course. About half past twelve?
Wife	Fine. And have you got any brochures on hotels in the city?
Travel agent	Well, we haven't got any brochures, but we've got some names and addresses of hotels. We can telex them, or you can write to them.
Wife	Fine, thanks.
Travel agent	Thank you very much.

Check!

1 Are there any planes to Mexico City on Sunday?
2 When do the planes leave?
3 What is the number of the evening flight?
4 What is the husband and wife's telephone number?

Language Focus

Making requests:

> Can you give me your telephone number, please?
> I'd like some information about . . .

Talking about availability:

Have you got	any brochures about hotels?
Are there	

Yes, we've got some	brochures.
No, we haven't got any	

Object pronouns:

Can you give **me** your phone number?		
Can I help **you**?		
Can you phone **us** tomorrow?		

I – me	it – it
you – you	we – us
he – him	they – them
she – her	

Talking about times:

	a quarter	past	nine.
There's a plane to Paris at	half		
	a quarter to		

The alphabet:

The flight to Copenhagen is **TR5234**

ABCDEFGHIJKLMN OPQRSTUVWXYZ

PRACTICE

1

A Can I help you?
B Yes, I'd like some information about flights to Bangkok.
A When would you like to fly?
B Are there any flights on Monday?
A Yes, there are two. One at half past nine and one at a quarter past eight in the evening.

Now you:
Ask your partner.

A	B
Bangkok / Monday?	9.30 am 8.15 pm
Santiago / Friday?	11.45 am
Moscow / Thursday?	8.00 am 12.15 pm 3.30 pm
Sydney / Saturday?	12.30 pm 1.30 pm

Toni Paull

Now you:
Make conversations with your partner like this:

A	B
Mr Greene?	4.30
Miss Davis?	2.00
Mrs Cameron?	3.45
Ms Jenkins?	11.15
Mr and Mrs Dale?	10.45

2

A Can I talk to Mr Greene, please?
B He's not here at the moment.
   Can you phone him again at half-past four?
A Okay. Thank you.
B That's all right.

3 Read this conversation with your partner.

A   Morning. Can I help you?
B   Yes. Have you got any apples?
A   Yes, we have. Would you like some?
B   I'd like six please.

Now ask for:

pineapples	grapefruit	melons
oranges	pears	lemons

4 SPELLING
A   What's your name?
B   Evans.
A   How do you spell that?
B   E — V — A — N — S

Now you:
Ask your partners how to spell their names.

5 Fill in the missing words from this list:
me, you, him, her, it, us, them.

a)   My number's 76253. Can you phone _me_ tonight?
b)   Sue is on the phone. Can you talk to _him_ ?
c)   We don't know Colchester. Can you help _us_ ?
d)   Where's my car? I can't find _it_ .
e)   The children are in the living room. Can you get _them_ ?
f)   You're very tired. Can I help _you_ ?
g)   Is Chris in his flat? I can't see _her_ .

6 SOUNDS   match /æ/ ~ much /ʌ/

Listen to the cassette and repeat these words with /æ/:

    man / flat / match

Listen again and repeat these words with /ʌ/:

    pub / Sunday / much

Now listen to the cassette and tick /æ/ or /ʌ/:

	1	2	3	4	5	6	7	8
/æ/								
/ʌ/								

TRANSFER

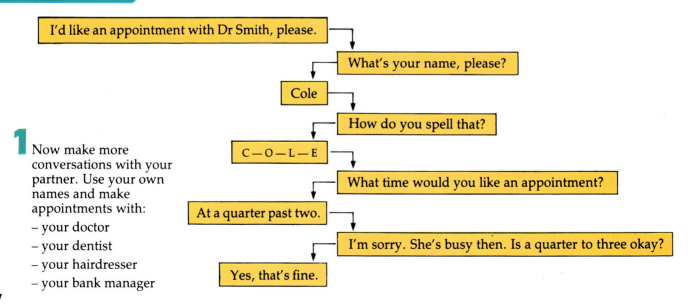

I'd like an appointment with Dr Smith, please.

What's your name, please?

Cole

How do you spell that?

C — O — L — E

What time would you like an appointment?

At a quarter past two.

I'm sorry. She's busy then. Is a quarter to three okay?

Yes, that's fine.

1 Now make more conversations with your partner. Use your own names and make appointments with:
– your doctor
– your dentist
– your hairdresser
– your bank manager

2

STUDENT A

You want hotel rooms for all your family: your mother and father, your sixteen-year-old sister, your brother and his wife, and yourself.
Ask your partner about the free rooms in the hotel. Are they single, double, with bath, with shower, with TV?.
I'd like a room for my mother and father. They'd like a double room with a bath.

STUDENT B

You have the information about the free rooms in the hotel.
Tell your partner what sort of rooms you have got.
We can give them Room 14. It's a double and it has a bath. Or we can give them Room 46. It's very quiet.

Hotel Majestic

Room Number	Single	Double	Bath	Shower	TV	Fridge	Quiet	SeaView
12			•		•	•		
13	•			•	•			•
14		•	•			•		•
22	•		•					•
25		•		•		•		•
28		•		•			•	
33		•		•			•	
39	•			•			•	
45	•			•	•		•	
46		•		•		•		
47		•	•					

3 🔊 **LISTENING**
Alan is at the airport. He wants some travel insurance. Listen to the conversation and then fill in the form.

Travel Insurance

Name:

Address:

Age: Flight number:

Destination:

Departure time:

Signature:

4 **WRITING**
Write a letter to the British Tourist Office in your country. You would like some information about holidays in South-West England.

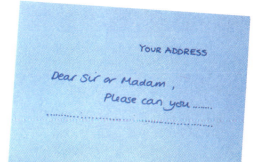

YOUR ADDRESS

Dear Sir or Madam,
          Please can you ....
....

Language Summary

Now you know how to:

- **Make requests:**
  I'd like some information about . . .
  Can you give me some brochures?

- **Talk about availability:**
  Are there any planes on Thursday?
  Have you got any rooms with a TV?

- **Use object pronouns:**
  I can phone him tomorrow.
  I'd like a room for them.

- **Talk about the time:**
  At a quarter past six.
  It's half past seven.

- **Use the alphabet to spell words and names:**
  My name's Smith.   S — M — I — T — H

1

Market Trader   Come on ladies and gentlemen. Who wants a bargain? Look at these fantastic new car radios. They're British and they're cheap.

Sarah   How much are they?

Trader   How much are they? In the shops they're £100. But I don't want £100. I don't want £75. I don't even want £50! Ladies and gentlemen, I want £40 for this stereo. Who wants one? Who's got £40?

Sarah   Me. Here's £40.

2

David   How much are those batteries?

Trader   The HP2s?

David   Yes.

Trader   They're 39p each. How many would you like?

David   Four, please.

3

Sarah   How much are these black jeans?

Trader   They're £21.50.

Sarah   And that green jacket?

Trader   It's £29.99.

Sarah   That's not bad, but I want a blue one really.

Trader   Sorry, love, I've only got this green one, or a red one.

Check!

1   In the market the car radio is
    a) £75.   b) £50.   c) £40.

2   In the shops the car radio is
    a) £100.   b) £75.   c) £50.

3   One HP2 battery is
    a) 49p.   b) 39p.   c) 29p.

4   The jeans are
    a) £20.50.   b) £21.50.   c) £20.

Asking and giving the price:

How much	is that red jacket? are those black jeans?	It's They're	£15.

How many:

How many batteries	do you want? would you like?	Four please.

Who: | Who wants a car radio? |

This/That:

This jacket That battery	is	£30. 99p.

These/Those:

These records Those batteries	are	£1.99 99p	each.

One:

I don't want a green jacket. Have you got a blue **one**? Look at this new car radio. Who wants **one**?

Colours:

yellow socks

black pullover

white shirt

blue jeans

red jacket

PRACTICE

SALE

£18.00 £15.00

£1.00 £9.99 £9.99 £8.99

1 Look at these pictures and ask for the prices of the clothes.

A How much are those blue jeans?
B They're £15.

2 Ask about the things in the picture like this:

A I'd like some postcards, please. How much are they?
B They're 6p each. How many would you like?
A Six, please.

3 Ask about the luggage:

A Who's got a red suitcase?
B John Howard.

4 Now ask the people in the picture about their luggage:

A Is this your suitcase, John?
B No, I've got a red one.

5 SOUNDS   bargain /g/ ~ jacket /k/

Listen to the cassette and repeat these words with /g/:

got / bargain / big

Listen again and repeat these words with /k/:

can / jacket / black

Now listen to the cassette and tick /g/ or /k/:

	1	2	3	4	5	6	7	8
/g/								
/k/								

TRANSFER

1 LISTENING

Sarah wants to buy some things for her flat. Listen to her conversation and write in the prices of the things.

Now you:
Talk to your partner about the things in the picture.

VAUXHALL Estate, 1980, dark blue, electric windows, 50,000 miles. £1,100 — 01-670 4501.

BMW 201, 1981, metallic blue, radio / cassette, electric windows, 28,000 miles. £4,584 — 01-328 0899.

CITROEN 2CV, 1980, dark blue, 60,000 miles. £750 — 01-578 3450.

VW GOLF, 1984, red, stereo, 30,000 miles. £2,000 — 01-621 0149.

FORD SIERRA, 1985, dark green, 40,000 miles, stereo. £2,500 — 01-621 7324.

HONDA CIVIC, 1985, dark brown, 40,000 miles, stereo. £2,500 — 01-224 6970.

2 READING

Choose one of these cars, but don't tell your partner your choice. Your partner asks questions to find out your choice. Here are some questions:

- How old is it?
- Is it a green one?
- Is the mileage 50,000?
- How much is it?
- Has it got a . . . ?

3

Ask the people in your class about their families:
- Have you got any brothers or sisters?
- How many . . . ?

4 WRITING

You want to sell something. Write an advertisement like this:

FOR SALE
AEG WASHING MACHINE
ONE YEAR OLD
£180
RING 62215

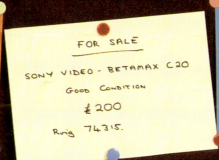

FOR SALE
SONY VIDEO - BETAMAX C20
GOOD CONDITION
£200
Ring 74315.

FOR SALE
OLIVETTI LETTERA 32 TYPEWRITER
£25
TEL: 68123

Language Summary

Now you know how to:

- **Talk about prices:**
  How much is that jacket? *It's £30.*

- **Talk about numbers:**
  How many batteries do you want? *Four, please.*

- **Ask WHO questions:**
  Who wants one?

1

Good afternoon everyone. It's ten past four and I'm here at Heathrow Airport where hundreds of people are waiting for the President and his wife. They're coming from New York on Concorde . . .

2

. . . well, we're all waiting and watching. Ah, the door's opening . . . Who's coming out? It's the President. And there's his wife. She's waving . . .

3

. . . they're walking to their car. But what's the President's wife doing? She's stopping and talking to people in the crowd . . .

4

. . . now at twenty-five to five they're leaving the airport in their car. So it's back to the studio. This is Andrew Brett at Heathrow.

What are you doing?

I'm waiting for the President.

Check! Fill in the missing words:

1 Hundreds of people are waiting at *Heathrow*
2 The President and his wife are coming from *New york*
3 They are coming on *Concorde*
4 The President's wife is talking to *people*

Describing actions:

What	are	you they	doing?	I'm You're She's We're They're	waiting for the President. standing here at Heathrow.
	is	she it		It's stopping.	

come	coming
leave	leaving
stop	stopping

Asking who: | Who's coming out? | It's the President. |

What's the time?

It's
five past ten
10.05

It's
ten past ten
10.10

It's
twenty past ten
10.20

It's
twenty-five past ten
10.25

It's
twenty-five to eleven
10.35

It's
twenty to eleven
10.40

It's
ten to eleven
10.50

It's
five to eleven
10.55

PRACTICE

1 Ask the people in the pictures what they are doing.

A What are you doing, Roger?
B I'm posting a letter.

2 Now ask your partner about the people in the photos.

A What are Ellen and Mark doing?
B They're watching TV.

3 What are the people doing?
Ask your partner.

- Who's that?
- What's she doing?
- Who's _____ ing?

MRS PETERS   MRS HALL   THE POSTMAN   MR GRUNDY   CATHY   OLIVER   NICHOLE

4

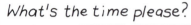

What's the time please?

It's five past seven.

5 SOUNDS   fourteen / forty

Listen to the cassette and repeat these -*teen* numbers:

13 14 15 16 17 18 19

Listen again and repeat these -*ty* numbers:

30 40 50 60 70 80 90

Now listen to the cassette and write down the numbers in these sentences:

1	2	3	4
5	6	7	8

TRANSFER

1 Find 5 differences between these two pictures.

2 LISTENING

Andrew Brett, the TV reporter, is describing a fire at a hotel.
Write down four things that are happening.

1	
2	
3	
4	

3 WRITING

It is half past nine in the morning and you
are at Southampton. You are waiting for a
famous person to arrive on the QE2.
Describe what is happening.

Megut.

It's half past nine in the morning and I'm standing here at Southampton docks

Thele

4 GAME

Think of more
actions to mime.

STUDENT A *Mime these actions*
a) washing your face
b) combing your hair
c) writing a letter
d) playing tennis
e) . . .
f) . . .

STUDENT B *Guess what your partner is doing*
You're reading!
No, you're writing.
You're writing a letter.

Language Summary

*Now you
know
how to:*

● **Describe actions:**

What are you doing?   *I'm waiting for my brother.*
What's she doing?   *She's talking to the reporters.*

● **Talk about times:**

What's the time, please?   *It's five past ten.*
It's twenty-five to one.

is programme (abshrlms ??)

1 Sarah Andrews writes for *The Colchester Gazette* and at the moment she is getting information for a newspaper story. She is talking to Colchester's Member of Parliament.

Sarah First of all, can I ask you about your job?

MP I work in the Houses of Parliament in London, of course, and also here in the town. Today I'm working in the Colchester office.

Sarah Tell me what you do every day? When do you start work?

MP From Monday to Friday I live in London, near Parliament. I have breakfast about 8.30, and start work at 9.30. I write letters, read papers and meet different people. Then I have lunch at about one o'clock. Parliament starts work at half past two, and we discuss the country's problems.

Sarah What do you do in the evenings?

MP I work! Parliament works in the evening, and we finish late. I get home between ten and twelve at night.

Sarah And what about the weekends?

MP Well, today's Saturday, and I'm working in Colchester. I'm meeting local people, and helping them with their problems.

2

Sarah is back in the office on Monday and her ed is reading her story about the MP.

Editor That's good, Sarah, but I want more *information*. Is he working in London today?

Sarah No, he isn't. Parliament isn't working this week. He's talking to a group of businessmen in Colchester.

Editor Well, go and listen to him. And ask more questions.

Check!

1 Who is Sarah interviewing?
2 Why is she asking questions?
3 Where does the MP work?
4 Where does the MP live?

Language Focus

The Present Continuous:

Is he	working in London today?	Yes,	he is. I am. they are.
Are you they		No,	he isn't. I'm not. they aren't.

I'm not	working today.
She isn't	
We You aren't They	

The Present Simple and the Present Continuous:	I work in London, but **today** I'm working in Colchester. Sarah writes for a newspaper, and **at the moment** she's writing about an MP.
Asking permission:	Can I ask you some questions?

PRACTICE

1 Ask your partner what the people are doing.

A   Is he playing squash?
B   No, he isn't. He's playing table tennis.
    No, he isn't playing squash. He's playing table tennis.

2 Make conversations like this with your partner. You are in Britain.

A   Where do you come from?
B   From Venezuela. I live in Caracas.
A   Where are you living at the moment?
B   I'm living in London.
A   . . .

Where / from?	What language / at home / in Britain?
Caracas / London	Spanish / English
Turin / Colchester	Italian / English
Paris / Cardiff	French / English

3 Federica is a skiing instructor in the winter and a windsurfing instructor in the summer. It is summer now.

Ask your partner about:
- What does she do in the winter?
- Where does she . . .?
- What is she doing now?

Winter
teach skiing
live in a flat
work in the mountains
drive a Snomobile

Summer
teach windsurfing
live in a tent
work on the beach
drive a boat

4 Here is a diet.
Ask your partner what he or she can eat.

THE SLIMFAST DIET

Eat yourself fit with the Six Week Slimplan

WEEK ONE

✗ NO	✓ YES
milk	water
apples	bananas
biscuits	brown bread
potatoes	carrots
whisky	wine
sausages	cheese
sugar	green vegetables
bread	yoghourt
bacon	salad
chocolate	fruit juice
cakes	fish
spaghetti	

5 SOUNDS   One or more?

🔲 Listen to the cassette and repeat this sentence about **one** person:

The student's playing football.

Listen again and repeat this sentence about **more than one** person:

The students are playing football.

Now listen to the cassette and tick **one** or **more than one**:

	1	2	3	4	5	6	7
One							
More than one							

TRANSFER

1 Interview your partners, and make a report on their work or studies.

Interview	1	2	3	4	5
Question:					
where / work?					
when / leave home?					
when / start work?					
when / lunch?					
when / finish?					
. . .					
. . .					

2 GAME

STUDENT A

what to do:
1. Sit back to back with your partner.
2. Tell him or her where you are.
3. Think of what you are doing but **don't** tell your partner.
4. Answer your partner's questions.

example:

I'm in a street in my town
I'm talking to a friend

No, I'm not.
Yes, I am.

STUDENT B

what to do:
1. Sit back to back with your partner.
2. Your partner tells you where he or she is.
3. Find out what your partner is doing.

example:

I'm in a street in my town.

Are you walking?
Are you talking to a friend?

3 LISTENING

Debbie and Mike are talking about their jobs. Write what they do and when.

	Debbie	Mike
in the morning in the afternoon in the evening	*get up at 6*	*read letters*

4 WRITING

You are on holiday in Wales. Write a postcard to friends. Tell them what you are doing. Say why it's different from what you do at home.

Language Summary

Now you know how to:

- **Describe what you're doing now:**
  I'm writing a story at the moment.
  He isn't working today.

- **Describe what you do and what you're doing:**
  I work in London, but I'm shopping in Colchester today.
  She works in London from Monday to Friday, but she's working in her garden in Colchester today.

- **Ask permission:**
  Can I ask you some questions?

Tony Laing is working on Stuart Wilson's boat at Bosham on the south coast of England.

Tony	This really is a nice boat you've got, Stuart. Do you usually come to Bosham in the summer?
Stuart	No, I usually take the boat to Spain. I've got friends there, and we sail around the Mediterranean in the summer. But I'm saving money this year, because I want to sail to Africa next year. I want to buy a navigation system as well, so I can sail in bad weather.
Tony	Why do you want to sail in bad weather? That's no fun!
Stuart	Well, I enjoy it. Why are you working in the summer?
Tony	I usually stay here in the holidays. I'm working on these boats so I can get some money. I want to buy a small boat.
Stuart	Well, you're doing a good job. Time for a break. Do you want a cup of coffee?
Tony	Yes, that's a good idea. Thanks.

Check!

1 Where is Tony working?
2 Why is he saving money?
3 Where does Stuart usually go in the summer?
4 What does Stuart want to buy?

Language Focus

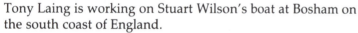

Describing what you usually do:

I	usually work in the summer.
I don't	

Giving reasons: *sebeb*

Why are you working here?	I'm working	**so** I can get	a new boat.
		because I want to buy	

Want:

I want to save some money.
Do you want to go for a drink?

1 Fiona isn't working today. She has the day off.

A What does she usually do at work?
B What is she doing today at home?

usually	*at the moment*
sit at a desk	lie on the sofa
drink coffee	eat an orange
write letters	read a magazine
eat a sandwich for lunch	have roast beef
work for eight hours	not work

2 John and Richard are working today, but it's Sunday and they are in New York.

A What do they usually do on a Sunday?
B What are they doing today?

usually	*at the moment*
play with their children	work hard
read the newspaper	talk about business
drink wine	drink coffee
have Sunday lunch	eat a sandwich
work in the garden	work in a hot office

3 Jane wants to go out with Pierre. She phones on Monday, Tuesday, Wednesday . . .

Monday

Jane	Do you want to go out?
Pierre	I'm sorry. I'm working.
Jane	Why are you working?
Pierre	I'm working so I can get some money for my holidays.

Now you make the conversations between Jane and Pierre for Tuesday, Wednesday, Thursday and Friday.

Tuesday
want to go for a drink?
learn English – get a better job

Wednesday
go to the cinema?
write to my bank – get a loan for a new car

Thursday
go to the theatre?
training – play football at the weekend

Friday
go to a disco?
wash my clothes – take Sally to a disco

4 SOUNDS   cheap /tʃ/ ~ Geoff /dʒ/

🎧 Listen to the cassette and repeat these words with /tʃ/:

cheap / kitchen / much

Listen again and repeat these words with /dʒ/:

Geoff / engineer / fridge

Now listen to the cassette and tick /tʃ/ or /dʒ/:

	1	2	3	4	5	6	7	8
/tʃ/								
/dʒ/								

TRANSFER

1 You are on holiday and talking to some new friends.
Find out about them.
Ask questions like this:

- What do you do?
- Where do you usually go on holiday?

Talk about sport, weekends, free time . . .

2 DISCUSSION
Ask seven friends what they want. Write a (✓) when they say 'yes'.

Do you want to:	1	2	3	4	5	6	7
live in a city?							
have a lot of children?							
be rich?							
have long holidays?							
work for forty years in one job?							

Ask them why they want or do not want to do these things.

3 WRITING
Write about what you want from your life.

I'm working in an office but I want to be a star....
I'm living in a flat, but I want .....

1 What does Peter Slater do?
2 When does he start work?
3 When does he finish work?
4 What does he do at home?
5 What is he writing a book about?
6 When can you buy his book?

A DAY IN THE LIFE OF

Peter Slater,
the presenter of a
breakfast
TV programme,
talks about his day.

My day starts very, very early. I get up at four o'clock in the morning. A taxi takes me to the studio, and then I have a cup of coffee and read the newspapers. The programme starts at six a.m. and I work with Jenny Morris. We read the news to people at home, and we talk to famous people, MPs, writers, and sportsmen and women. It's a lot of fun but hard work.

The programme finishes at nine o'clock, but I can't go home. I work in the office from nine to lunchtime. I write things for the TV programme the next morning. There is a lot of work, and I drink cups and cups of coffee. About one-fifteen I have a quick lunch in the canteen, usually just a sandwich.

In the afternoon I can go home, and I usually sleep for two or three hours. Then I start work at home. I'm writing a book at the moment, and so I sit in my office and work. I usually write one book a year. At the moment I'm writing about tennis stars.

You can buy it next year!

Language Summary

*Now you
know
how to:*

• **Describe what you usually do:**

I usually work in London, but I'm working here today.

• **Give the reason why:**

I'm working here today because I want to save money.

• **Say what you want:**

I want to get my own boat and sail to America.

STUDENT A – TRAVELLER   Student B cover this page

You are in London and you want to go to the Republic of Ireland for a few days. You are talking on the phone to the tourist office, and you want to get some information about travel – the fares, the times, the sorts of transport.

Questions to ask:
- How much does it cost?
- Is there a ferry from Holyhead to Cork?
- How long does it take?
- What days can I travel?
- What time does it leave?
- What's the phone number?

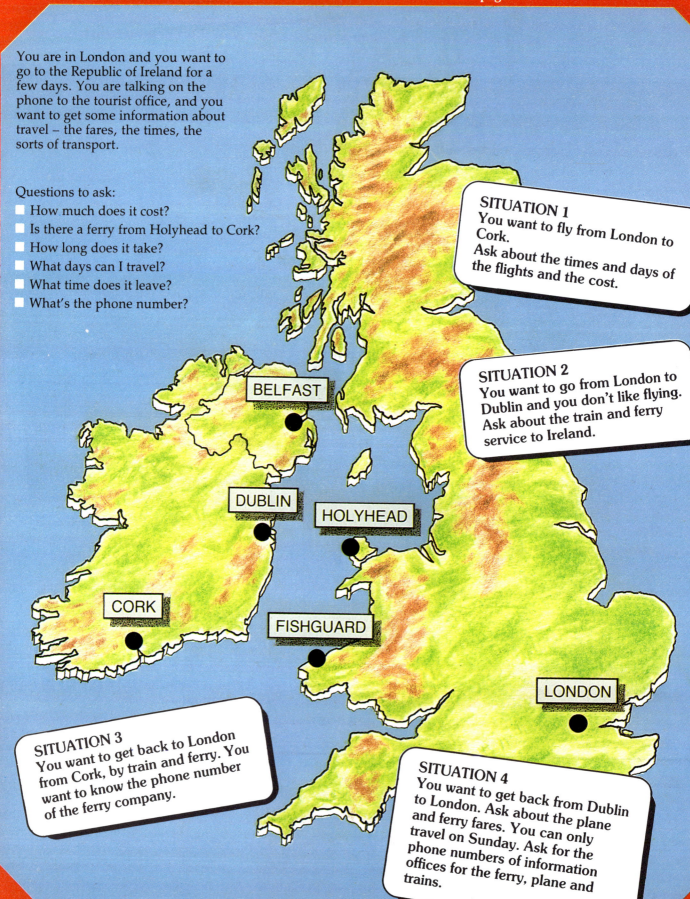

SITUATION 1
You want to fly from London to Cork.
Ask about the times and days of the flights and the cost.

SITUATION 2
You want to go from London to Dublin and you don't like flying. Ask about the train and ferry service to Ireland.

SITUATION 3
You want to get back to London from Cork, by train and ferry. You want to know the phone number of the ferry company.

SITUATION 4
You want to get back from Dublin to London. Ask about the plane and ferry fares. You can only travel on Sunday. Ask for the phone numbers of information offices for the ferry, plane and trains.

BELFAST

DUBLIN

HOLYHEAD

CORK

FISHGUARD

LONDON

TRAVELLING TO IRELAND

You haven't got a map of Ireland, but you have the travel information that your partner wants. If you don't understand where he or she wants to go, ask a question.

BY AIR

	London–Cork	London–Dublin	Dublin–London	Cork–London
fare:	£65	£63	£63	£65
journey:	1 hour	1 hour	1 hour	1 hour
days:	Mon–Sat	Mon–Sat	Mon–Sat	Mon–Sat
times:	11.30	12.00	10.00	9.30
tel. no:	01-576-7843	01-576-7843	488-2397	507666

BY SEA

	Fishguard–Cork	Cork–Fishguard	Holyhead–Dublin	Dublin–Holyhead
fare:	£10	£10	£15	£15
journey:	9 hours	9 hours	3½ hours	3½ hours
days:	Mon–Wed–Fri	Tu–Thu–Sat	every day	every day
times:	8.00	8.30	10.30	16.00
tel. no:	043-4590	507666	023-3911	541-8329

TRAINS IN BRITAIN

	London–Fishguard	Fishguard–London	London–Holyhead	Holyhead–London
fare:	£25	£25	£30	£30
journey:	4 hours	4 hours	3½ hours	3½ hours
days:	every day	every day	every day	every day
times:	12.00	14.00	5.30	20.30
tel. no:	01-635-1111	01-635-1111	01-635-1111	01-635-1111

International telephone codes: UK 0044
Ireland/Eire 00353

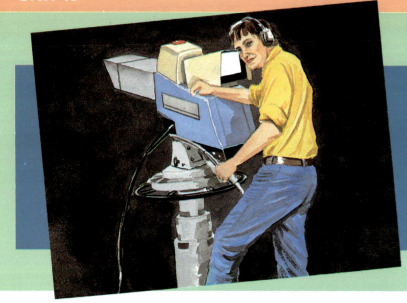

My name's Charlie and I work as a cameraman for a big television company in Birmingham. It's a good job, but we work long hours, and at weekends too. I work on popular TV programmes, so I meet famous people. This week we're making a new comedy programme.

WHAT DO

My name's Helen. I'm married and I've got two children, a boy and a girl. I work in London as a computer operator for a big tobacco company. It's not very interesting work. I sit in front of a computer in an office all day and send customers their accounts. I'd like to change jobs and work in a hotel or an airport.

LISTENING
Gary Hawkins is talking to a newspaper reporter about his job.

Questions	Answers
What does Gary do?	
Where is Radio North Sea?	
What four things does Gary do?	
How long does he live on the ship?	
How long does he live in his flat?	
Where is the flat?	

My name's Jenny. I work in the theatre in Washington D.C. I'm not an actor – I work behind the scenes. I help with the lights and with the costumes. I build and paint the scenery. It's an interesting job and I meet very interesting people. This week we're doing Shakespeare's *Hamlet*.

THEY DO ?

My name's George. I'm single and I live in Manchester. I'm an estate agent – I sell houses. I take photographs of houses and put them in my office window. People come and look at the photos. If they're interested in a particular house, I tell them about it and take them to see it. Today I'm showing people my house. I'm buying a new one in the country.

DISCUSSION

What makes a good job?

What is important for you?

- a lot of money
- interesting work
- long holidays
- working with other people and helping them
- a place of work near your home
- friendly people to work with

Now discuss these ideas with your partner.

WRITING

Write a letter to one of these four people and tell them about yourself – where you live, your job or studies, and what you do in your free time.

Dear....
Thank you for your

UNIT 17 Quantities

1

"Goodbye everyone."

"Have a good flight."

"Thanks for everything."

"Send us a postcard from the States."

2

Roger	You haven't got any time to buy presents. The plane leaves at six o'clock, you know.
Ellen	There's plenty of time, Roger, and there aren't many things on our list.
Mark	Okay, but we haven't got much English money left.
Sue	What do you want to buy?
Ellen	All sorts of things for our friends and family at home. Here's the list . . .
Roger	Ten Shetland wool pullovers! That's rather a lot.
Mark	Well, we have a lot of friends.
Roger	Six metres of tartan material!
Sue	Tartan?
Ellen	Yes, people love real Scottish tartan. It's very expensive in the States.
Roger	Souvenirs of London? Surely you've got enough souvenirs.
Mark	We've got plenty, but these are for our family.

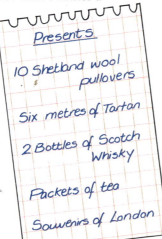

Presents

10 Shetland wool pullovers

Six metres of Tartan

2 Bottles of Scotch Whisky

Packets of tea

Souvenirs of London

Check! Right or wrong? (✓ or ✗)

1 Ellen and Mark are returning to the United States by air. ☐

2 · They haven't got enough time to buy presents. ☐

3 They've got plenty of English money. ☐

4 They want to buy things for their English friends. ☐

5 They want to buy a lot of pullovers. ☐

Language Focus

Quantities:

Have you got enough	time? money? presents?	Yes, we've got	enough plenty of a lot of	time. money. presents.
		No, we haven't got	enough any	

A lot of / much / many:

There's We've got	a lot of	tea. time.	There isn't We haven't got	much money. many presents.

Of:

Twenty packets		tea.
Six metres	of	tartan.
A bottle		Scotch whisky.

Large numbers 100 to 1,000,000:

100	a / one hundred
1000	a / one thousand
1,000,000	a / one million

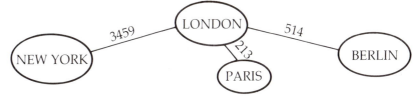

Paris is two hundred and thirteen miles from London.

Berlin is five hundred and fourteen miles from London.

New York is three thousand four hundred and fifty-nine miles from London.

PRACTICE

MOUSSAKA RECIPE
250g butter
6 onions
4 aubergines
50g flour
250ml milk
150g cheese
2 eggs
½kg minced lamb

1 You and your partner want to make Moussaka for a party.

What you have got:
500g butter
2 onions
1 aubergine
1kg flour
100ml milk
No cheese
10 eggs
250g minced lamb

Make a conversation like this:

A We want two hundred and fifty grams of butter. Have we got enough?

B Yes, we've got a lot of butter. There's five hundred grams.

2 Make sentences about the pictures like this:

● There aren't many cars in the car park.

cars / car park

orange juice / glass

matches / matchbox

milk / bottle

cigarettes / packet

people / street

3 Make conversations about
the drinks list.

A What do you want to drink?
B A cup of coffee. What about you?
A A glass of wine, please.

BEVERAGES

Coffee.................................35p

Tea.................................22p

Milk.................................25p

CocaCola.................................35p

Orange juice.................................40p

Mineral water.................................30p

Hot Chocolate.................................45p

4 Ask your partner questions like this:
A How far is it from London to Aberdeen?
B Four hundred miles.
A That's about six hundred and forty kilometres.
B How much is the train fare?
A It's forty-four pounds.

From London to:	Miles / kilometres	Train fare
Aberdeen	400/ 640	£44.00
Paris	200/ 320	£29.00
Berlin	593/ 954	£59.90
Rome	908/ 1461	£66.60
Athens	1501/ 2415	£107.30
Madrid	755/ 1214	£67.80

5 SOUNDS   vet /v/ ~ wet /w/

Listen to the cassette and repeat
these words with /v/:

vet / save / television

Listen again and repeat these words with
/w/:

wet / weather / Stockwell

Now listen to these pairs of words.
Write two letters for each pair /v+w/ or /w+w/ etc:

1	2	3	4	5	6	7	8

TRANSFER

1 You and your partner are going on a
camping holiday with two friends.
Here are some of the things you have
got.

Talk about what you have got and
what you want to buy for the holiday.

A We've got plenty of toothpaste, but
we haven't got enough
toothbrushes. We've only got two.
B So we need two toothbrushes.
What about clothes and things to
eat with?

Continue the conversation and then
make a list of the things you want
to buy.

2 LISTENING

Here are four short conversations.
Are the sentences about them right or wrong?

CONVERSATION A
1 There are a lot of people in the bar.
2 Mary wants a glass of wine.

CONVERSATION B
1 The driver buys a lot of petrol.
2 He hasn't got enough oil in his car.

CONVERSATION C
1 The woman has got plenty of money.
2 The man has got plenty of money.

CONVERSATION D
1 There's plenty of sugar.
2 There isn't much butter left.
3 There aren't many eggs.

4 WRITING

Write a letter to a friend.
Write five sentences about
your town or school
or college.

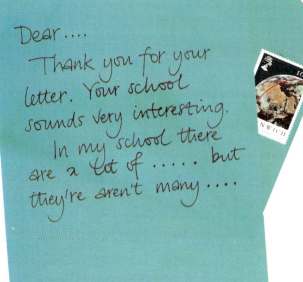

Dear ....
Thank you for your letter. Your school sounds very interesting.
In my school there are a lot of ..... but they're aren't many ....

3 READING

AN ENGLISHMAN'S HOME IS HIS CASTLE

For many British people, a house is the most important thing in their lives. In fact, about 60% of the population do not rent their homes from other people, but have their own homes. But prices are going up all the time, and many young people have not got enough money to buy a house. They live in small flats or in their parents' house, even when they are married.

Prices are especially high in the South-East of England. In the North, and in Scotland, prices are quite low, but in London a two-bedroom house can cost £40,000. A three-bedroom house can cost £60,000 or more. That's a lot of money for a young couple and they have to save for several years to get the money. First, they need a deposit - usually 10% of the price of the house.

Young people often buy old houses, perhaps more than a hundred years old, because they are not so expensive. But they have to spend a lot of time and money on repairs and decoration. Every British town has several 'Do-It-Yourself' shops, where people buy the things they need for the jobs around the house.

5 GAME

There are eight food and drink words in this puzzle.
But there are nine letters left. These letters make one
of the things in the Moussaka on page 64.

K	L	I	M	A	E	E
C	W	I	N	E	G	G
B	H	M	B	E	G	G
R	B	E	E	I	G	G
E	E	A	E	A	N	N
A	E	E	U	S	T	T
D	R	T	R	E	E	E

1

Roger Rosemary, our Washington office needs a new manager. We want the right person for the job so I'm going to do the interviews myself. Can you book me a flight please?

Rosemary Certainly, Mr Eastwood. When are you going to leave?

Roger On Tuesday morning. That's the 27th of May. I'm going to fly from Heathrow.

Rosemary And when are you going to come back?

Roger Let me look at my diary. The interviews are on Wednesday and Thursday. On Friday I'm going to meet everyone in the Washington office, and on Saturday I want to see the city. So, can you get me a return ticket for Sunday, please?

Rosemary Sunday, fine.

2

David Do you know? Roger's going to spend a week in America.

Chris Lucky Roger! What about Sue?

David She isn't going to go. She's going to stay with her sister in Aberdeen.

Check! Fill in the missing words in the sentences:

1 Roger is going to fly to _America_ next _week_.
2 He is going to leave from _Heathrow_ airport.
3 He is going to _meet_ people for the manager's job in the Washington office.
4 On _Friday_ he wants to meet everyone in the office.
5 Sue is going to stay with her _sister_ in Aberdeen.

Talking about plans:

When	are you is he	going to come back?	On	Monday morning. Tuesday. Wednesday afternoon.

I'm You're She's We're They're	going to	go shopping tomorrow. do the work today. clean the car this weekend.

I'm not He isn't We aren't	going to do it today.

Ordinal numbers:

1st	2nd	3rd	4th	5th	6th	7th	8th	9th	10th
first	second	third	fourth	fifth	sixth	seventh	eighth	ninth	tenth

JANUARY

Monday		2	9	16	23	30
Tuesday		3	10	17	24	31
Wednesday		4	11	18	25	
Thursday		5	12	19	26	
Friday		6	13	20	27	
Saturday		7	14	21	28	
Sunday	1	8	15	22	29	

FEBRUARY

Monday		6	13	20	27
Tuesday		7	14	21	28
Wednesday	1	8	15	22	29
Thursday	2	9	16	23	
Friday	3	10	17	24	
Saturday	4	11	18	25	
Sunday	5	12	19	26	

MARCH

Monday		5	12	19	26	
Tuesday		6	13	20	27	
Wednesday		7	14	21	28	
Thursday	1	8	15	22	29	
Friday	2	9	16	23	30	
Saturday	3	10	17	24	31	
Sunday	4	11	18	25		

APRIL

Monday		2	9	16	23	30
Tuesday		3	10	17	24	
Wednesday		4	11	18	25	
Thursday		5	12	19	26	
Friday		6	13	20	27	
Saturday		7	14	21	28	
Sunday	1	8	15	22	29	

MAY

Monday		7	14	21	28	
Tuesday	1	8	15	22	29	
Wednesday	2	9	16	23	30	
Thursday	3	10	17	24	31	
Friday	4	11	18	25		
Saturday	5	12	19	26		
Sunday	6	13	20	27		

JUNE

Monday		4	11	18	25	
Tuesday		5	12	19	26	
Wednesday		6	13	20	27	
Thursday		7	14	21	28	
Friday	1	8	15	22	29	
Saturday	2	9	16	23	30	
Sunday	3	10	17	24		

JULY

Monday		2	9	16	23	30
Tuesday		3	10	17	24	31
Wednesday		4	11	18	25	
Thursday		5	12	19	26	
Friday		6	13	20	27	
Saturday		7	14	21	28	
Sunday	1	8	15	22	29	

AUGUST

Monday		6	13	20	27
Tuesday		7	14	21	28
Wednesday	1	8	15	22	29
Thursday	2	9	16	23	30
Friday	3	10	17	24	31
Saturday	4	11	18	25	
Sunday	5	12	19	26	

SEPTEMBER

Monday		3	10	17	24
Tuesday		4	11	18	25
Wednesday		5	12	19	26
Thursday		6	13	20	27
Friday		7	14	21	28
Saturday	1	8	15	22	29
Sunday	2	9	16	23	30

OCTOBER

Monday	1	8	15	22	29
Tuesday	2	9	16	23	30
Wednesday	3	10	17	24	31
Thursday	4	11	18	25	
Friday	5	12	19	26	
Saturday	6	13	20	27	
Sunday	7	14	21	28	

NOVEMBER

Monday		5	12	19	26
Tuesday		6	13	20	27
Wednesday		7	14	21	28
Thursday	1	8	15	22	29
Friday	2	9	16	23	30
Saturday	3	10	17	24	
Sunday	4	11	18	25	

DECEMBER

Monday		3	10	17	24	31
Tuesday		4	11	18	25	
Wednesday		5	12	19	26	
Thursday		6	13	20	27	
Friday		7	14	21	28	
Saturday	1	8	15	22	29	
Sunday	2	9	16	23	30	

PRACTICE

May	Morning	Afternoon	Evening
Monday 26	OFFICE	OFFICE	PARTY AT OFFICE 8pm
Tuesday 27	LEAVE HEATHROW AIRPORT 11·30am	ARRIVE IN WASHINGTON D.C. 1pm	SEE WASHINGTON WITH JACK EDWARDS
Wednesday 28	MEET OLD MANAGER JACK EDWARDS 10·00am	INTERVIEWS 2·00pm 4·00pm	DINNER WITH THE NEW MANAGER
Thursday 29	INTERVIEWS 9·00am 11·00am	MEETING TO CHOOSE THE NEW MANAGER	OFFICE PARTY FOR THE NEW MANAGER
Friday 30	DISCUSS THE JOB WITH EDWARDS	AND THE NEW MANAGER ALL DAY	
Saturday 31	WRITE REPORT OF VISIT TO WASHINGTON	SHOPPING	ARRIVE HEATHROW 8·00pm
Sunday 1	LEAVE WASHINGTON 8·00am		

1 Here is Roger's diary for next week.

You work with Roger and you are talking to him about his week in Washington.

A What are you going to do on Wednesday morning, Roger?
B I'm going to meet Jack Edwards.

Continue the conversation with your partner. Ask about the other days of the week.

2 Talk about Roger's week in Washington.

A When is Roger going to leave England?
B He's going to leave at half-past eleven on Tuesday.
A What date's that?
B It's the twenty-seventh of May.

Continue the conversation with your partner.

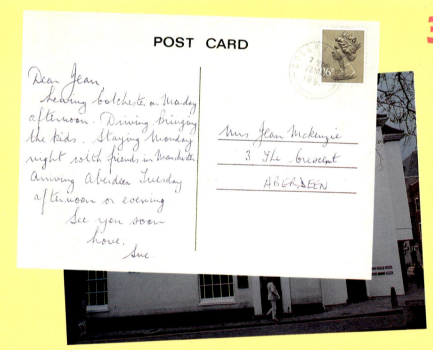

POST CARD

Dear Jean
Leaving Colchester on Monday afternoon. Driving bringing the kids. Staying Monday night with friends in Manchester. Arriving Aberdeen Tuesday afternoon or evening
See you soon
love,
Sue.

Mrs Jean McKenzie
3 The Crescent
ABERDEEN

3 This postcard is from Sue Eastwood to her sister, Jean, in Aberdeen. But Jean doesn't get the postcard. She telephones Sue and asks her some questions. Write in Sue's answers.

Sue Hello, Colchester 84620, Sue Eastwood here.
Jean Hello Sue. It's Jean. How are you?
Sue Fine. And you?
Jean Look, are you going to come up next week?
Sue Yes, we are. We're . . .
Jean Good. Are you going to come by train?
Sue No, . . .
Jean And the children. Are you going to bring them with you?
Sue Yes . . . but . . .
Jean I see, so when are you going to get here?
Sue On . . .
Jean Is Roger going to come?
Sue No. . . .

4 SOUNDS   who /uː/ ~ how /aʊ/

Listen to the cassette and repeat these words with /uː/:

who / you / new

Listen again and repeat these words with /aʊ/:

how / down / about

Now listen to the cassette and tick /uː/ or /aʊ/:

	1	2	3	4	5	6	7	8
/uː/								
/aʊ/								

June	Morning	Afternoon
Monday 9		
Tuesday 10		
Wednesday 11		
Thursday 12		
Friday 13		
Saturday 14		
Sunday 15		

1 🔘🔘 LISTENING

Roger Eastwood and John Bellinger are talking on the phone. Write what Roger is doing on each day of the week. Fill in the missing information in the pages of the diary.

2 WRITING

Make a diary about your plans for next week.

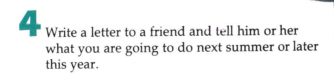

	Morning	Afternoon
Monday		
Tuesday		
Wednesday		
Thursday		

3

Ask your partners about their coming week. Answer their questions about your plans.

4

Write a letter to a friend and tell him or her what you are going to do next summer or later this year.

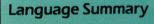

Language Summary

Now you know how to:

- **Talk about plans:**

  When are you going to come back?   *On Tuesday.*

  Is Sue going to fly to America?   *No, she isn't.*

  What are you going to do on Friday?   *I'm going to see a film.*

- **Talk about dates:**

  Monday 5th October. (*It's Monday, the fifth of October.*)

  Wednesday 9th January. (*It's Wednesday, January the ninth.*)

Dear Sue, Jake and Rachel,
I'm having a very busy time in the States, but it's a great place! Everything is big and new. The cars are bigger than British cars, the buildings are taller, and the cities are busier than our cities. But the Americans are really friendly people, friendlier than the British! The weather is awful this week. It's as bad as our English weather.

See you on Saturday
Love Roger

Mrs Sue Eastwood,
7, Royal Terrace,
COLCHESTER,
ESSEX,
ENGLAND. CO1 2BP

Check!
1 Where is Roger?
2 Who is he writing to?
3 What is different in America?

DO YOU KNOW? DO YOU KNOW? DO YOU KNOW?

The tallest twins in the world are Dan and Doug Busch of Arizona, USA.

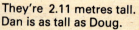

They're 2.11 metres tall. Dan is as tall as Doug.

The longest suspension bridge in the world is 1410 metres long. It's the Humber Bridge near Hull, UK.

The world's smallest bird is the bee humming bird.

The largest hotel in the world has 3200 rooms. It's the Hotel Rossiya in Moscow.

Check!
1 What is special about the Hotel Rossiya in Moscow?
2 How long is the Humber Bridge? 1410 metres
3 Who are the tallest twins in the world?

DO YOU KNOW? DO YOU KNOW? DO YOU KNOW?

Comparing two different things:	American cars are bigger than British cars. American people are friendlier than British people.

Comparing two things that are the same:	The weather in Washington is as bad as our English weather. Doug Busch is as tall as Dan Busch.

Comparing more than two things:	The Humber Bridge is the longest suspension bridge The Rossiya Hotel is the biggest hotel Doug and Dan Busch are the tallest twins	in the world.

tall	taller	tallest
long	longer	longest
big	bigger	biggest

busy	busier	busiest
friendly	friendlier	friendliest

PRACTICE

1 A Which mountain is higher, The Eiger or The Matterhorn?
B The Matterhorn. But which is the highest mountain in Europe?
A Mont Blanc is.

The Eiger 3973 metres	The Matterhorn 4481 metres	Mont Blanc 4807 metres

Now you
Talk to your partner.

Rivers – *long*	The Thames 346 km	The Shannon 386 km	The Amazon 6437 km
Airports – *big*	Heathrow 1,140 hectares	Gatwick 759 hectares	King Abdul Aziz 29,784 hectares
Buildings – *tall*	The Post Office Tower 189 m	Big Ben 96 m	The Sears Tower 443 m

	Andrew	Louise	Fred	Jenny	Sandra	Simon
Age	23	24	72	59	24	36
Height	1.95 m	1.70 m	1.45 m	1.68 m	1.78 m	1.75 m
Weight	79 kg	65 kg	50 kg	87 kg	56 kg	63 kg

2 Talk about the people in the picture.

A Who's the youngest person in the group?
B Andrew's the youngest.
A And who's the oldest in the group?
B It's Fred. Fred's the oldest.

Some useful words

short	shorter	shortest
fat	fatter	fattest
old	older	oldest
heavy	heavier	heaviest
small	smaller	smallest
thin	thinner	thinnest
young	younger	youngest

3 SOUNDS   cheap /tʃ/ ~ shop /ʃ/

Listen to the cassette and repeat these words with /tʃ/:

cheap / kitchen / watch

Now listen again and repeat these words with /ʃ/:

shop / washing / finish

Now listen to these pairs of words.
Write two letters for each pair eg /tʃ + ʃ/ or /ʃ + ʃ /

1	2	3	4	5	6	7	8

1 Fill in your details on this chart.

Now fill in your partner's details.
Ask these questions:
- How old are you?
- How tall are you?
- How much do you weigh?

Now in pairs talk about the people in your survey.

	NAME	AGE	HEIGHT	WEIGHT
You				
Partner 1				
Partner 2				
Partner 3				
Partner 4				

2 WRITING
Write about some of the people in your class. Who is the oldest, the youngest, the tallest?

3 Make up a quiz about your country or town. Write two kinds of questions:
- Which is larger, _____ or _____?
- Which is the largest _____ in _____?

4 SPOT THE DIFFERENCE
Find 5 differences between the two pictures.

Now you know how to:

- **Compare two or more things:**
  Which airport is larger, Gatwick or Heathrow?   *Heathrow is larger than Gatwick.*
  The weather in Washington is as bad as the weather here.
  The Rossiya Hotel is the largest in the world.

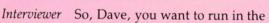

Interviewer	So, Dave, you want to run in the London marathon this year?
Dave	Yes, that's right. I was in a half-marathon last year, and I want to do a full marathon this year.
Interviewer	Is it very difficult?
Dave	Well, you need a lot of energy. But anybody can do it, if they train hard.
Interviewer	What do you do to get ready? How often do you train?
Dave	I usually train for two hours a day. I always go running before breakfast.
Interviewer	What about in the evening?
Dave	It depends. I often go for a long run after work. And at the weekends I run about fifteen kilometres a day, sometimes twenty to thirty kilometres.
Interviewer	Do you ever get fed up with running? Do you ever want to do something different?
Dave	Of course. I often get angry about the time I spend on training, but I'm looking forward to the marathon, so I'm happy to work for it.
Interviewer	Do you think running is good for you?
Dave	Yes. Running is good for everybody. Everybody needs exercise, and running is easy and healthy.

LOCAL MAN IN LONDON MARATHON

There were about 20,000 runners in this year's London Marathon yesterday. One of them was Dave Harper from Colchester. He usually teaches at the English Centre but yesterday he was a marathon runner . . .

Check!

1 When does Dave go running?
2 How many kilometres does he run at the weekend?
3 What does he do before work?

Describing routines:

When do you do your training?	I	always usually often sometimes	go running before breakfast.

Do you ever	get fed up get bored	with training?	Yes,	I do. I often do.
			No,	I don't. I never do.

Past tense of the verb BE:

I he she was it	you we were they

Everybody, anybody, somebody, nobody:

It's not difficult. Anybody can do it.
It's very difficult. Nobody can do it.
It's very popular. Everybody wants to do it.
It's the telephone. Somebody wants to talk to you.

PRACTICE

1 Ask your partner to describe
Paul and Cathy's routines.

A   What does Paul usually do in the morning?
B   He usually . . .

often

usually

sometimes   *always*

usually

often

sometimes

always

76

2 Here are the programmes for Damian Long's and The Pictures' last tours. Ask your partner questions like this:

A Where was Damian on Friday 2nd?
B He was in Chichester, at the Festival Theatre.
A When were The Pictures in Liverpool?
B On 4th March.

DAMIAN LONG

* LONDON *

Dominion Theatre
TOTTENHAM COURT ROAD

Mon 12 Sept at 8pm

September

Fri 2 CHICHESTER Festival Theatre
Sat 3 SOUTHEND Cliffs Pavillion
Sun 4 MANCHESTER Free Trade Hall
Tue 6 NEWCASTLE City Hall
Wed 7 LIVERPOOL Empire Theatre
Thurs 8 NOTTINGHAM Sherwood Room
Fri 9 CROYDON Fairfield Halls
Sat 10 PLYMOUTH Theatre Royal
Sun 11 POOLE Arts Centre

THE PICTURES
UK TOUR

March

2 SLOUGH Thames Hall
3 BIRMINGHAM Odeon
4 LIVERPOOL Empire
5 MANCHESTER Apollo
6 PRESTON Guild Hall
7 SHEFFIELD City Hall
8 NEWCASTLE City Hall
9 EDINBURGH Playhouse
10 ABERDEEN Capitol

3 SOUNDS   white /aɪ/ ~ wait /eɪ/

Listen to the cassette and repeat these words with /aɪ/:

white / tonight / sometimes

Now listen again and repeat these words with /eɪ/:

wait / say / information

Now listen to these pairs of words.
Write two letters for each word /eɪ+aɪ/ *or* /aɪ+aɪ/ etc:

1	2	3	4	5	6	7	8

TRANSFER

1 'Milestones in History'
Where were you at these important times in history?
A Where were you in . . .?
B I was at . . .

Charles and Di marry
29 July 1981

9 December 1980
Lennon shot in New Yor

21 JULY 1969
Armstrong walks on the moon

Russians boycott Olympics
8 May 1984

Nixon Resigns
8 AUGUST 1974

13 May 1981
POPE SHOT

2

Ask your partner about him or herself.
- What do you usually do at the weekends?
- Where do you usually go for your holidays?
- Do you ever play sport?

a politician   a rock star

3

GAME
Think of a famous person

Don't tell your partner the name. He or she asks questions to find out the name of the person.
Ask and answer questions like this:

| Do you ever | work outside?
go to America?
sing in nightclubs? | I | always
usually
often
sometimes
never | . . . |

an actor   a writer

4

WRITING
Describe your own routine on a normal day. What do you usually do? Where do you usually go?

5

WRITING
What do you think about the British and the Americans? Write sentences like this:
- The British always queue for things.
- The Americans always drive big cars.

Language Summary

Now you know how to:

- **Describe routines:**
  I usually work in the evenings.
  She always runs at the weekend.
  We never get fed up with running.
  They often go to the cinema.

- **Talk about the past:**
  There were 20,000 runners.
  He was in London.

- **Talk about people:**
  Everybody was there.
  Anybody can do it.

Washington Monument

Jeff. Memorial

Capitol

NASA Museum

Simon Welcome back, Roger. Did you have a good trip?

Roger Yes, thanks. It was very good. I worked hard, but I had a good time as well.

Simon What did you do in Washington?

Roger Well, I was very busy. I talked to a lot of people in the office and asked a lot of questions. Then I interviewed some people for the job and appointed the new office manager.

Simon And were you busy in the evenings too?

Roger Yes, I was. Sometimes I worked, and then had dinner with friends, or I went to the cinema.

Simon Which places did you visit? Did you see the White House, the Senate, and so on?

Roger Yes, I did. I went sightseeing on Saturday and visited the famous places. I went to the NASA Museum and that was fantastic. They had the Apollo spaceship, from the moon trip. It looked very small. I'm glad I wasn't in it!

Simon So, you liked the States.

Roger Yes, I did. I loved the people and the food, but not the weather, it was too hot. But it was a good trip.

Check!

1 Where did Roger go?
2 Why did he interview some people?
3 Did he visit the White House?
4 Which museum did he go to?
5 Did he like the States?

Language Focus

Talking about the past:

Was the weather good?	No, it wasn't.
Were the people friendly?	Yes, they were.

Did	you / he / they	see the sights?	Yes,	I / he / we / they	did.	I / He / We / They	saw	the Capitol. / the White House.

What did	you / she / they	do there?	I / She / We / They	visited a lot of friends. / worked hard.

Which places did you visit?	I went to the Capitol and the White House.

Verbs in the past:

A regular verb – play	An irregular verb – have
I You He played . . . She We They	I You He had . . . She We They
work – worked walk – walked visit – visited	see – saw go – went fly – flew

PRACTICE

1

Your partner is back from a business trip to New York. Here's his or her diary. Ask what he or she did on Monday, Tuesday, Wednesday in New York.

A What did you do on Monday morning?
B I went to . . .

	Morning	Afternoon	Evening
Monday	Go to Wall St.	Meet Mr. Hooper	Dinner with the Hoopers.
Tuesday	Call New York Times	Lunch with some journalists	Play squash with Jim
Wednesday	Write sales report	Fly to Washington	Go to Opera in the Kennedy Centre.

2

When he or she was in the United States, your partner also visited Washington, Chicago, Los Angeles and San Francisco. Ask what he or she did there?

A Where did you go after New York?
B I went to . . .
A What did you see there?
B I . . .

Disneyland, Los Angeles.

The White House, Washington.

View from Sears Tower, Chicago.

Baseball game, San Francisco.

3 Ask your partner what he or she thought about America.

A What did you ~~like~~
love about America?
~~dislike~~ + _бередіменіъ_

B I ~~liked~~
loved the . . .
~~hated~~

use these words:

hamburgers	taxis	ice-cream	baseball
beer	policemen	weather	TV
people	museums	traffic	countryside

4 SOUNDS   Full and reduced sounds in verbs

🔘🔘 Listen to the cassette and repeat these sentences with **full** verb sounds:

CAN   Can you swim?
WAS   Was he a doctor?

Now listen again and repeat these sentences with **reduced** verb sounds:

CAN . I can swim
WAS   He was a doctor

Now listen to these sentences and tick *full* or *reduced*:

		full	*reduced*
1	HAS		
2	CAN		
3	HAVE		
4	WAS		

		full	*reduced*
5	WAS		
6	HAD		
7	CAN		
8	HAS		

TRANSFER

1 Read this conversation

Now talk to your partner about a weekend in a town you know or about a weekend in an English town.

Oxford

Cambridge

Manchester

London

Did you have a good weekend in Brighton?

Yes thanks, I did. I had a lot of fun.

What did you do there?

I visited a lot of friends, and I went to the cinen

Oh, which film did you see?

I saw the new Superman film.

Was it good?

Yes, I loved it.

Where did you go in Brighton?

I went to the shops and I had lunch in a pub near the sea.

2 Interview two or three of your partners. Ask them what they did last week.

Write their answers and make a report to the other people in your class.

3 Ask your partner about an important day in his or her life.

- What happened?
- What did he or she do?
- Where were they?
- What did he or she think about it?

Ask about your partner's

— first day at school.
— first day at work.
— wedding day.
— eighteenth birthday.

4 **ROLE PLAY**
You and your partner are back home after two years in different countries.
Ask and answer questions about:

the people   the work   the buildings   the weather   the sights   the food   the countryside

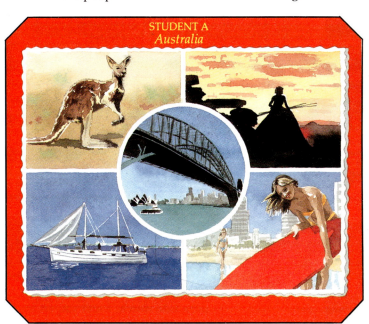

STUDENT A
Australia

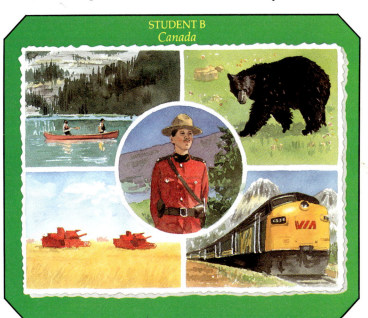

STUDENT B
Canada

Police find body of wife

Cambridge police found the body of missing housewife Mrs Jean King yesterday. The body was in a field outside the town. Mrs King disappeared from her home in Sanderson St on July 25th. Her husband saw her for the last time at six o'clock that day, and then she disappeared. "Perhaps she went for a walk," said her hus-band. The police worked hard on the mystery for six weeks. They interviewed over three thousand people and searched the river and in the nearby forest. Yesterday a farmer telephoned the police and said there was something in his field. Now the police want to know: who did it?

5 **READING**
1 When did Mrs King disappear?
2 Where did they find her body?
3 How many people did the police talk to?
4 Where did the police look for Mrs King?

6 **WRITING**
Write about something important that happened in your town or city. Give details about the time and place.

Language Summary

Now you know how to:

● **Ask and talk about things in the past:**
What did you do?   *I went to Washington.*
Did you see the White House?   *Yes, I did.*
Which film did you see?   *We saw Superman.*

● **Use regular and irregular verbs in the past:**

play – played	have – had	eat – ate	find – found
work – worked	go – went	take – took	fly – flew
arrive – arrived	see – saw	think – thought	be – was/were

82

1

Sarah Morning Geoff. Did you enjoy your holiday in Wales?
Geoff Yes thanks. We had a great time.
Sarah Where did you stay? In a hotel?
Geoff No, we didn't. We took our tent into the mountains, near Snowdon. We cooked all our meals on an open fire and ate outside.
Sarah Sounds wonderful. Was the weather good?
Geoff Fantastic. The sun shone nearly every day and it didn't rain once.
Sarah Did you like the people?
Geoff Yes, they were great. We met some Welsh farmers in the pub. They spoke Welsh with their friends, but of course they knew English too.
Sarah When did you get back? Last night?
Geoff No, I think we were crazy. We came back this morning. We got up at 4.30, left at 5 and arrived here at 9. I'm exhausted. What about you? Did you have a good weekend?
Sarah Yes, but I didn't do much. I just stayed in. The weather was terrible.

2

Becky Hi, Chris. Did you have a good time in London?
Chris It was okay. I went to the David Bowie concert at Wembley.
Becky Really. What did you think of it? Did you enjoy it?
Chris Not much. We stood outside in the rain, and there were too many people. I didn't enjoy it very much. I thought the music was too loud.
Becky A lot of concerts are like that.
Chris So, what did you do at the weekend?
Becky I went to see the new Meryl Streep film. I thought it was a bit long, but it had a very good story.

Check!

1 Where did Geoff go for his holiday?
2 What was the weather like?
3 When did he come back from holiday?
4 What did Chris do at the weekend?
5 Did Becky like the new Meryl Streep film?

Language Focus

Talking about the past:

What did you do at the weekend?	I / We	didn't do much.

Asking about and giving opinions:

Did you	like / enjoy	the concert?

Yes,	it was fantastic. / very much.
	It was okay.
No,	not much / I didn't.

What did you think of it?	I liked it very much. / I thought it was very good. / I didn't enjoy it very much.

Some irregular verbs:

Present	Past
shine	shone
meet	met
speak	spoke
know	knew
come back	came back
get up	got up
leave	left
stand	stood

PRACTICE 1

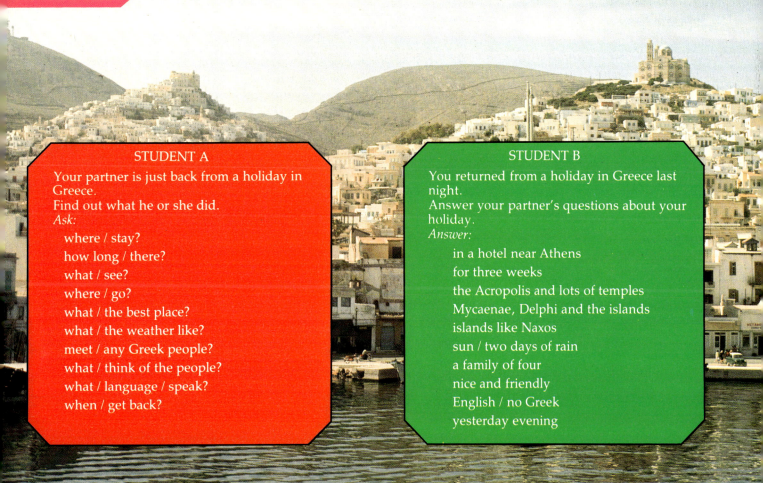

STUDENT A

Your partner is just back from a holiday in Greece.
Find out what he or she did.
Ask:

where / stay?

how long / there?

what / see?

where / go?

what / the best place?

what / the weather like?

meet / any Greek people?

what / think of the people?

what / language / speak?

when / get back?

STUDENT B

You returned from a holiday in Greece last night.
Answer your partner's questions about your holiday.
Answer:

in a hotel near Athens

for three weeks

the Acropolis and lots of temples

Mycaenae, Delphi and the islands

islands like Naxos

sun / two days of rain

a family of four

nice and friendly

English / no Greek

yesterday evening

2 You were outside a large shop when a bomb went off. The police arrived and wanted
to know what happened. Answer their questions.

Police Where were you when the bomb went off?
You I . . .
Police When did it go off? Did you notice the time?
You Yes . . .
Police Where was the bomb, do you think?
You It . . . , I think.

Police Who was near the door at the time?
You There . . .
Police And what did they do when the bomb went
You They all . . .
Police How many people were hurt, do you know?
You Yes, . . .

3 Here are some of the things you and
your partner went to see last week.
Ask and answer questions like this:

A What did you think of . . .?
B I thought . . .

A Did you | like
           | enjoy | the . . .?

B Yes, it was . . .
   No, . . .

4 SOUNDS   simple past endings /t/, /d/, /ɪd/

🔊 Listen to the cassette and repeat these
words with the ending /t/:

  worked / talked / looked

Listen again and repeat these words with
the ending /d/:

  interviewed / played / loved

Listen again and repeat these words with
ending /ɪd/:

  visited / started / ended

Now listen to the cassette and tick /t/, /d/ or /ɪd/:

	1	2	3	4	5	6	7	8
Ending /t/								
Ending /d/								
Ending /ɪd/								

TRANSFER

1 LISTENING

Jane is talking about when she got married. Write down what happened, and at what time it happened.

TIME?	WHAT HAPPENED?

2

Find out how your partners spent their free time last week. Ask questions about:

– number of evenings out
– to the cinema
– to the theatre
– books
– sports
– meals out
– TV

3

Last weekend you and your partner went to London. Here are some of your photos of the places you visited. Ask your partner what he or she thought of them.

THE MARKET – COVENT GARDEN

THE CUTTY SARK – GREENWICH

THE NATIONAL THEATRE – SOUTH BANK

THE THAMES BARRIER – WOOLWICH

A CHINESE MEAL – SOHO

KARL MARX'S TOMB – HIGHGATE CEMETERY

4 WRITING

Write about a recent holiday. Write where and when you went, where you stayed, what you visited and saw, what you did, and what you liked.

Language Summary

Now you know how to:

● **Talk about the past:**

I didn't | stay in a hotel.
| do very much.

● **Ask and give opinions about the past:**

Did you | like | the . . .? | Yes, it was great.
| enjoy | | No, not much.

What did you think of the . . .? | I thought it was . . .
| I didn't like it very much.

● **Use irregular verbs in the past:**

speak – spoke   spend – spent   leave – left

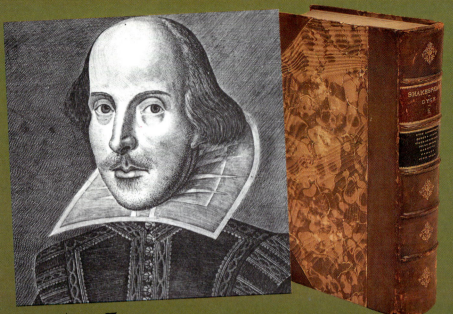

William Shakespeare was born in Stratford on April 23rd, 1564. His father, John Shakespeare, was an important man in the town – William did not come from a poor family.

When he was eighteen, William married Anne Hathaway in Stratford. But he didn't want to stay there. He wanted to be an actor and the best theatres were in London. So, in 1587 William went to London where he worked as an actor in a theatre called *The Rose*.

He began to write plays for the actors. He wrote *Romeo and Juliet*, *Julius Caesar*, *Richard II*, *Antony and Cleopatra*, and many more. Everyone liked his plays, and he became famous.

When James I became King in 1603, Shakespeare worked for him, and performed his plays for the King and his friends. He also worked at the famous Globe Theatre. This theatre presented his last play, *Henry VIII*. There was a gun in this play, and fire from the gun burned the theatre down.

In 1610 Shakespeare went back to Stratford. He wanted to live there with his family. But on April 23rd, 1610, William Shakespeare died. He was only forty-six years old.

NAME	Grace Kelly
BORN	1929
PLACE OF BIRTH	Philadelphia, USA
FIRST FAMOUS	after films in the 1950's
FILMS	'High Noon' 'High Society'
MARRIED	Prince Rainier of Monaco, 1956
DIED	in a car crash in France, 1982

Grace Kelly was born in 1929 in Philadelphia. She was an actress and first became famous in the early 1950's. She made famous films like 'High Society' and 'High Noon'. In 1956 she married Prince Rainier of Monaco, and she went to live in Monte Carlo. She had three children and died in a car crash in France in 1982.

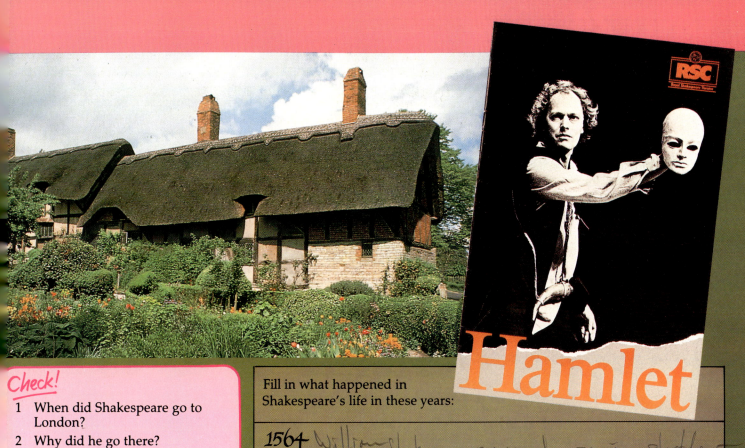

Check!

1 When did Shakespeare go to London?

2 Why did he go there?

3 What was the name of the first theatre he worked in?

4 How did the Globe Theatre burn down?

5 What was Shakespeare's wife's name?

6 How old was Shakespeare when he got married?

Fill in what happened in Shakespeare's life in these years:

1564	William Shakespeare was born in Stratford
1582	
1587	William went to London
1603	Shakespeare worked for James
1610	William Shakespeare died

Now write the biographies of David Niven and Jimi Hendrix

NAME	*David Niven*
BORN	*1910*
PLACE OF BIRTH	*Abingdon, England*
FIRST JOBS	*Journalist and salesman*
FIRST FAMOUS	*after the film 'Bachelor Mother' in 1938*
FILMS	*'Around the World in Eighty Days' 'The Pink Panther'*
DIED	*1983, Switzerland.*

NAME	*Jimi Hendrix*
BORN	*1942*
PLACE OF BIRTH	*Seattle, USA*
FIRST JOB	*soldier in the US army*
FIRST FAMOUS	*after the hit single 'Hey Joe' in 1967*
RECORDS	*'Purple Haze' 'Voodoo Chile'*
DIED	*1970, London.*

1

Editor Sarah. I've got some extra work for you, I'm afraid.

Sarah Oh? What's that?

Editor The Employment Minister, Neil Watkins, is coming to Colchester on Sunday. He's speaking at the Town Hall. I want you to go and listen, report his speech, and then interview him.

Sarah I'm sorry, John. I can't do it. I'm going away for the weekend. I have to go to my cousin's wedding on Saturday in Bristol.

Editor Well, nobody else can do it, and you're the best interviewer we've got. Do you have to stay until Sunday?

Sarah I don't have to, but it's difficult to get back.

Editor We can pay your train fare.

Sarah Okay, but I have to call my mother.

2

Sarah Hello. Hello Mother? It's Sarah . . . I'm fine. Listen, I've got some bad news for you. I can[ ]stay on Sunday. I've got to come back to wor[ ]. . . I'm sorry but I didn't know about it. I tol[ ]my boss about the wedding, but he said I hav[ ]to come back on Sunday morning . . . yes, I'[ ]afraid I have to, because everybody is on holiday or working on other stories . . . well, perhaps I can come earlier then, on Friday. Then I can help you . . .

Check!

1 Sarah is going to _____ at the weekend.
2 She is going to her cousin's _____.
3 _____, the Employment Minister, is speaking in Colchester on Sunday.
4 The editor wants Sarah to come back to _____ on _____.
5 The editor can _____ Sarah's train fare to help.

Language Focus

Expressing obligation:

I have I've got	to go to a wedding.
Do you have Have you got	to stay until Sunday?
I had to work last weekend.	

The Present Continuous tense with future meaning:

He's speaking on Sunday.
I'm going to a wedding on Saturday.

Giving reasons:	I can't work at the weekend, because I'm going away.

Expressing regret:	I'm sorry I can't do it. I can't do it, I'm afraid.

Talking about possibility:	We can repair your car next week. I can't do it – I'm going away.

PRACTICE

Ask your partner what you have to do.

A What do I have to do to get a job?
B First, you have to go to the Job Centre and show your work permit.
A And then?
B Then you have to fill in a form, and look at the list of jobs.

Getting a job

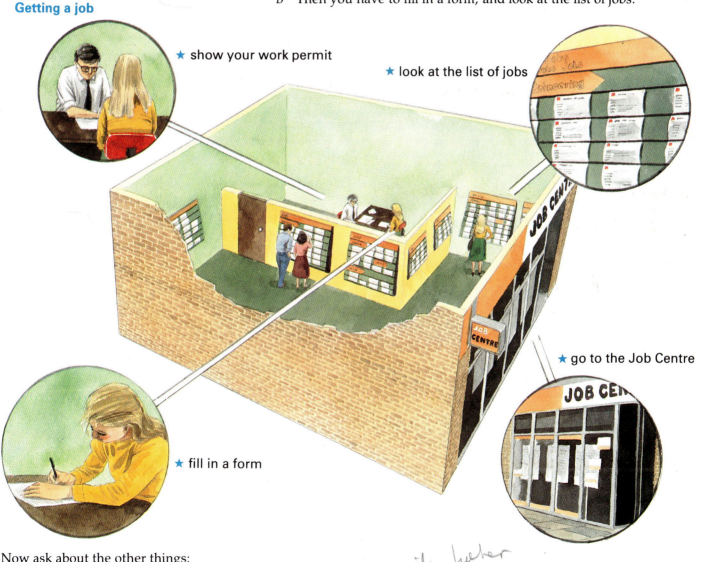

★ show your work permit

★ look at the list of jobs

★ go to the Job Centre

★ fill in a form

Now ask about the other things:

Renting a room   ★ buy a newspaper   ★ look at the advertisements   ★ call the interesting ones   ★ visit the house

Getting a TV licence ★ go to the Post Office   ★ fill in a form   ★ pay £46

Now ask again, with a different question:

What have I got to do . . . ?

2 Your partner wants you to do these things. Say you're sorry but you can't.
A   Can you help me with my work now?
B   I'm afraid I can't. I've got to go to the doctor's.

STUDENT A
Ask your partner

    help me with my work now
    give me a lift to London tomorrow
    help me repair my car this afternoon
    help me move my furniture on Sunday
    come to dinner tonight

STUDENT B
Give a good reason to your partner

    go to the doctor's
    visit my parents
    wash my hair
    write some letters
    do my washing

3 Here are Neil Watkins' plans for some of next week
Ask your partner what Neil Watkins is doing next week.

A   What's he doing on Wednesday?
B   He's giving a speech in the morning in Cardiff and then . . .

```
                        - 2 -

   Wednesday      give speech in Cardiff in the morning.
                  speak in the House of Commons in the evening.

   Thursday       have lunch with the Energy minister.
                  answer letters
                  go to the theatre in the evening.

   Friday         meet political journalists in the morning.
                  write an article for The Times newspaper.

   Saturday       speak in Manchester at 11 am.
                  have lunch with the Mayor of Manchester.
                  speak at a Trade Union dinner in the evening.

   Sunday         answer questions on a TV programme at 1 pm.
                  give interviews to some European journalists.
                  visit parents for dinner.
```

4   **SOUNDS**   think /θ/ ~ this /ð/

Listen to the cassette and repeat these words with /θ/:

    think / Heathrow / thanks

Listen again and repeat these words with /ð/:

    this / brother / that

Now listen to the cassette and tick /θ/ or /ð/:

	1	2	3	4	5	6	7	8
/θ/								
/ð/								

Read this advertisement and answer the questions.

1 How old does the new marketing manager have to be?

2 When does he or she have to start?

3 Which languages does he or she have to speak?

4 Does he or she have to travel?

MARKETING MANAGER

We're looking for a new Marketing Manager for an international company.
The right person has to be 28 to 35 and dynamic. He or she has to speak French, German and English, has to be happy about travelling to North America, Africa and the Far East. The Marketing Manager has to find new markets for our products and new products for old markets.

Is this you?
Can you start work in October?
Write to Box 23KL

AS

TEM

01- 246

WRITING
Write an advertisement for your job or a job you know about.

3 Interview your partners. Ask them about their past jobs or studies.
- What did they have to do?
- Was it good or bad?

Write a report on the information your partners give you.

Arrange a meeting with your partner for next Tuesday, Wednesday or Thursday. Make a diary for these days, with lots of plans in it. Don't show it to your partner. Now arrange a meeting on the telephone. Ask:

- What are you doing on . . .?
- Can we meet on . . .?
- Are you free on . . .?

1

Sue It's getting late Roger, it's raining and we haven't got a spare tyre. What are we going do?

Roger We could stop another car and ask the driver for help.

Sue I'm not very keen on that. Why don't we find phone box and call a garage instead?

Roger Yes, okay, that's a more sensible idea. Come on. Let's phone a garage.

2

Mechanic What's the problem? Can I do anything to help?

Roger I hope so. We've got a puncture.

Mechanic Well, why don't you change the wheel?

Sue That's the most sensible idea, but unfortunately we haven't got a spare.

Mechanic I see. Look, shall I take you to the garage in my van? You could bring the wheel, buy a new tyre and then I could bring you back here.

Roger That's very kind of you. Are you sure?

Mechanic Yes, of course. That's my job.

Check! Fill in the gaps with words from the dialogue:

1 Roger and Sue haven't got a _puncture_ tyre for their car.
2 They call from a _garage_.
3 The mechanic says, 'Why don't you _change_ the wheel?'
4 Sue and Roger are going to the nearest _garage_
5 They are going to buy a new _tyre_.

Language Focus

Making suggestions:

We could Let's	phone the garage.	

Why don't	we you	stop another car and ask for help?

Offering to do something for someone:

Can I do anything to help?
Shall I take you to the nearest garage?

Comparing with more and the most:

Roger Sue The mechanic	has	a sensible a more sensible the most sensible	idea.

brror vet uck

You are in Britain and are trying to
decide what presents to buy for your
friends and family.

A   What can I get for my sister?

B   Why don't you buy her an LP?
        or
      You could get her a scarf.   *buy a boiti*
                                     esop

Choose something to take home to
your mother and father, brothers
and sisters, and your best friends.

2 You are in a restaurant with a friend.
You don't know what to have.

A   What do you suggest?
B   Why don't we try roast lamb?
A   No, I'm not very keen on that.
B   Well, we could have . . .
Finish the conversation.

3 Your partner has a problem. Offer to help.

A   Can I do anything to help?
B   Yes, please. I'm going to be late for work.
A   Shall I give you a lift?
B   That's very kind of you. Thanks.

STARTERS

VEGETABLE SOUP
SMOKED MACKEREL
EGG MAYONNAISE

MAIN COURSE

ROAST LAMB
PIZZA
FRIED PLAICE

DESSERT

FRESH FRUIT SALAD
CHOCOLATE MOUSSE
BROWN BREAD ICECREAM

	problem	*offer*
1	late for work	give you a lift
2	need some shopping	go to the supermarket
3	no money	lend you £5
4	can't find my car keys	help you look for them
5	want to write a letter but can't type.	type it for you

4 Compare these people and things.

a) Important writers:
    Jane Austen – Charles Dickens – William
    Shakespeare.
    Jane Austen is an important writer. Charles
    Dickens is more important, but William
    Shakespeare is the most important writer.

b) Famous tennis players:
    Ivan Lendl – Martina Navratilova – John
    McEnroe.

c) Tiring sports:
    badminton – squash – swimming

d) Expensive perfumes:
    Rive Gauche – Givenchy – Chanel No 5.

5 SOUNDS   Noun plurals

Listen to the cassette and repeat this
sentence with plural /s/:

CIGARETTE   Have you got any
             cigarette**s**?

Now listen and repeat this sentence with
plural /z/:

KEY   Have you got my key**s**?

and this sentence with plural /ɪz/:

PEACH   Have you got any peach**es**?

Now listen to these sentences and tick /s/, /z/, or /ɪz/:

	1	2	3	4	5	6	7	8
/s/								
/z/								
/ɪz/								

TRANSFER

1 Read this
conversation.

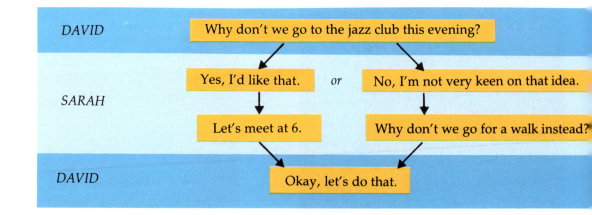

DAVID   Why don't we go to the jazz club this evening?

SARAH   Yes, I'd like that.   *or*   No, I'm not very keen on that idea.

         Let's meet at 6.   Why don't we go for a walk instead?

DAVID   Okay, let's do that.

Make your own
conversations using
these ideas:

suggestions	alternatives
go to cinema	. . .
. . .	go to the sports centre
have a snack	. . .

2 ROLE PLAY

The four people in your group all work in the same office. Your boss is very unfriendly to you all, and you want to do something about it. Discuss what you can do? Here are some ideas.

A thinks it is best to be friendly to your boss.

B thinks it is best to write a letter to the managing director.

C thinks it is best to go on strike.

D thinks it is best to find a job in another department.

Now write a short report of your discussion.

3 LISTENING

In each of these three conversations, someone has a problem and someone else makes helpful suggestions.
What are the problems and what are the suggestions?

	Problem	Suggestion	
Conversation A		1	
		2	
Conversation B		1	
		2	
Conversation C		1	
		2	

4

Compare these three buildings.

Language Summary

Now you know how to:

- **Make suggestions:**

  Why don't we change the wheel?

  I could phone the garage.

  Let's stop another car.

- **Offer to do something for someone:**

  Can I do anything to help?

  Shall I take you to the garage?

- **Compare with MORE and THE MOST:**

  famous   **more** famous   **the most** famous

  interesting   **more** interesting   **the most** interesting.

14, Chapel Lane
Hathersage
Derbyshire

Dear Chris,

Greetings from the cold North! Hope you are well and working hard in Colchester. We're getting ready to have a housewarming party – all the work is finished now. Would you like to come up for the weekend? We're planning to have the party on the 25th. That's a Saturday – and on the Sunday we're going to go sailing to Ladybower Reservoir. Would you like to bring a friend? You could bring Becky from Royal Terrace......

Please call and let me know if you'd like to come.

Yours
Carol.

Check!

1 Where does Carol live?
2 What is happening on the 25th?
3 Where is Carol going on the 26th?

Carol	Hello, 49367.
Chris	Hello Carol. It's Chris.
Carol	Hi, Chris. How are you?
Chris	I'm fine. Listen – thanks for your letter. I'd love to come up for the weekend. It's just what I need.
Carol	Great. Now, can you sail? I have to organise the boats for the weekend.
Chris	No, I can't, but I can learn!
Carol	Okay. And what about tennis? Can you play? We want to have a competition.
Chris	Well I like playing tennis, but I'm the worst player in the world.

Check!

1 Can Chris play tennis?
2 Can he sail?
3 Is he going to Derbyshire for the weekend?

Invitations:

Would you like to	come up for the weekend? go sailing on Sunday?	Yes,	I'd	love to. like that.
		That's a nice idea.		
		I'm sorry	I can't come on Sunday. I have to work tonight.	
		Sorry, I can't, but thanks anyway.		

Ability:

Can you	sail? play tennis?	Yes, I can. No, I can't.

Comparing:

I'm	a bad tennis player. a worse player than John. the worst player in the world.	He's	good. better. the best.

-ING forms:

We want to go sail**ing**. Do you like swimm**ing**? I like play**ing** tennis.

PRACTICE

1

Finish this phone conversation with your partner.

Nigel   Hello, 9844.
Becky Hello, Nigel. It's me, Becky.
Nigel   Oh hello Becky.
Becky Listen, would you like to go to a party on Saturday? We're going to have one here.
Nigel   Yes, I would love to. What time does it start?
Becky Oh, come about half past eight.
Nigel   I will, see you soon. Bye.

2 You are inviting your friend to go on holiday. Your friend accepts and makes some new suggestions.

A Would you like to go away for a few days?
B Yes, I'd love to. Let's go to Cambridge.
A That's a good idea.

Invitations	Suggestions
go away for a few days	Cambridge
go camping this weekend	Wales
learn windsurfing	go on Saturday
spend the summer in Greece	visit the smaller islands

3

Frank Hazzard interviews famous people on TV. He is on the phone now. He's inviting you to be on breakfast television next week. Accept or refuse his invitation.

Frank Would you like to talk about your new book on TV next week?
You   I'm sorry, I can't. I have to fly to Rome.

Invitations	*Reasons for refusing*
talk about your new book	have to fly to Rome
sing one of your new songs	have to work in the studio
talk about the government	have to see the President
talk about your new film	have to meet the director

drive

draw

sailing

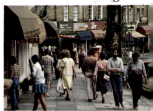
horse-riding

play chess

play the guitar

swimming

shopping

sew

type

fishing

sightseeing

4 Ask your partner

A   Can you drive?

B   Yes, I can.
    No, I can't.

5 Talk to your partner

A   Shall we go sailing at the weekend?

B   Yes, I'd love to. I like sailing.
    No, I don't like sailing.

6 SOUNDS   I like / I'd like

🔊 Listen to the cassette and repeat this request or wish:

I like that red pullover.
(*This means* I think it's nice.)

Listen again and repeat this statement:

I'd like that red pullover.
(*This means* I want it *or* Can I have it?)

Now listen to the cassette and tick **like** or **-'d like**:

	1	2	3	4	5	6	7	8
Like								
-'d like								

TRANSFER

1 Ask your partners what they like doing at the weekend. Ask about the best things to do at the weekend.

2 Find out what your partners think about film stars, pop groups, TV programmes, places to go and food.

THE BEST!
1
2
3
4
5

THE WORST!
1
2
3
4
5

You are on the telephone and are inviting your partner to dinner.

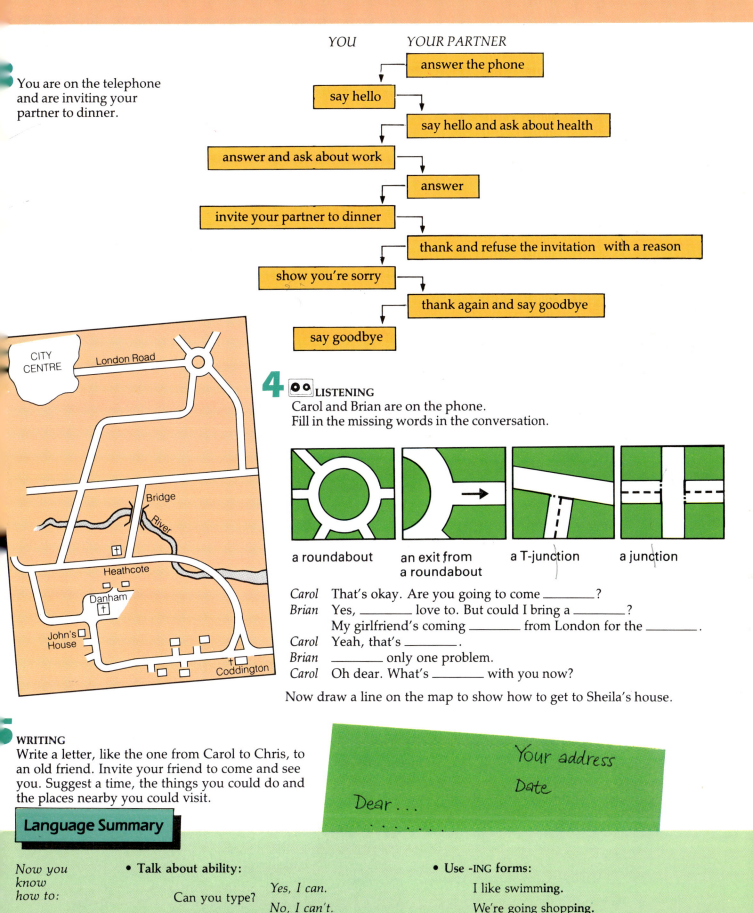

YOU   **YOUR PARTNER**

answer the phone

say hello

say hello and ask about health

answer and ask about work

answer

invite your partner to dinner

thank and refuse the invitation with a reason

show you're sorry

thank again and say goodbye

say goodbye

CITY CENTRE — London Road

Bridge

River

Heathcote

Danham

John's House

Coddington

4 🔲 **LISTENING**

Carol and Brian are on the phone.
Fill in the missing words in the conversation.

a roundabout   an exit from a roundabout   a T-junction   a junction

Carol   That's okay. Are you going to come _____?
Brian   Yes, _____ love to. But could I bring a _____?
     My girlfriend's coming _____ from London for the _____.
Carol   Yeah, that's _____.
Brian   _____ only one problem.
Carol   Oh dear. What's _____ with you now?

Now draw a line on the map to show how to get to Sheila's house.

WRITING

Write a letter, like the one from Carol to Chris, to an old friend. Invite your friend to come and see you. Suggest a time, the things you could do and the places nearby you could visit.

Your address

Date

Dear...
....

Language Summary

Now you know how to:

- **Talk about ability:**

     Can you type?   *Yes, I can.*
                         No, I can't.

- **Make, accept and refuse invitations:**

     Would you like to come and see me?   *Yes, I'd love to.*
                                              I'm sorry, I can't.

- **Use -ING forms:**

     I like swimming.
     We're going shopping.

1

Becky	Sarah, can you come here a minute?
Sarah	What's the problem?
Becky	I need some help. The TV isn't working and I'm missing the news.
Sarah	The plug probably needs a new fuse.
Becky	I think I've got one. Yes, here you are. And a screwdriver. Okay watch me, Becky. First, take the old fuse out and throw it away. Then put the new one in and screw the cover back on the plug. Don't forget that! Okay?
Becky	Great. Thanks.
Sarah	Well, switch on the TV. There you are. Right, I've got to go now. Don't be late for work!

2

David	My car's using too much petrol. It's costing me a fortune.
Sue	I saw a notice yesterday about petrol.
David	Really? What did it say?
Sue	You must use the right grade of petrol, and make sure your engine is correctly tuned.
David	Is that all?
Sue	Well, no. You mustn't drive too fast and you mustn't brake too hard.
David	Everyone says I drive too fast, and I don't often have to brake hard. Perhaps I need a new car.

SAVE PETROL NOW

Do's

Make sure your engine is correctly tuned

Check the air in your tyres

Use the right grade of petrol

Don'ts

Don't drive too fast

Don't brake too hard

Don't carry unnecessary weight

Check!　Right or wrong? (✓ or ✗)

1　Becky wants to watch the evening news. ☑
2　Sarah hasn't got time to help Becky. ☒
3　The plug is okay. ☒
4　David's car uses too much petrol. ☑
5　David never brakes too hard. ☒

Giving instructions:

| Watch me. Do it yourself! | You must | use the right grade of petrol. check the air in your tyres. |

| Don't forget to do that. | You mustn't | drive too fast. brake too hard. |

Need:

| I you we they | need | some help. |
| he she | needs | |

PRACTICE

1
A I want to change the hours. What must I do?
B First press this button here once. Then hold this button until it shows the hour you want.

Ask your partner how to change the minutes, seconds, and alarm.

Use these words:

minutes   button twice
seconds   button three times
alarm   button four times

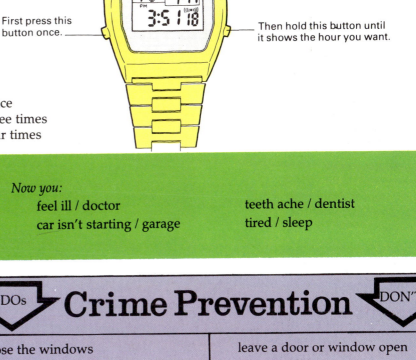

First press this button once.

Then hold this button until it shows the hour you want.

2 Talk to your partner like this:

A I feel ill.
B Well, you must go to the doctor.

Now you:

feel ill / doctor
car isn't starting / garage

teeth ache / dentist
tired / sleep

3 You are going away next Sunday for a week's holiday. You want to make sure your house is safe. Read the list of Do's and Don'ts.

Now finish the conversation with your partner.

A I'm going on holiday next week. What must I do?
B You must close your windows.
A Okay, what about doors?
B You must . . .
A . . .?

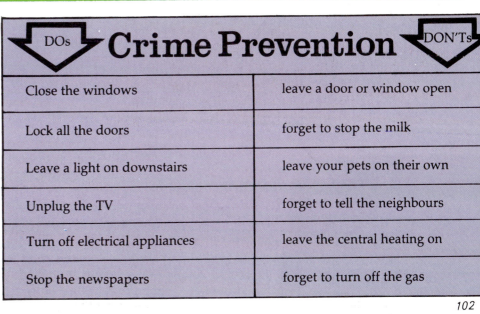

DOs Crime Prevention	DON'Ts
Close the windows	leave a door or window open
Lock all the doors	forget to stop the milk
Leave a light on downstairs	leave your pets on their own
Unplug the TV	forget to tell the neighbours
Turn off electrical appliances	leave the central heating on
Stop the newspapers	forget to turn off the gas

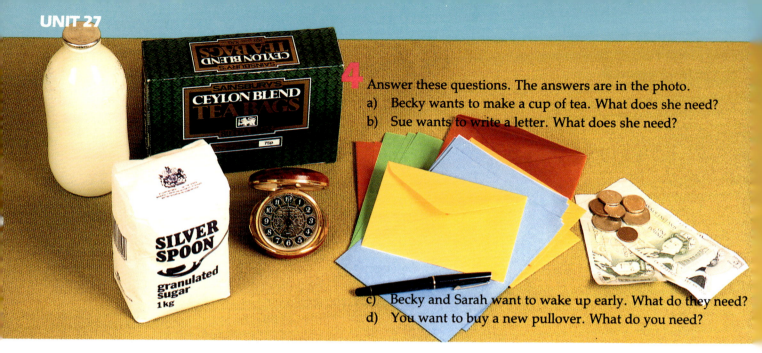

4 Answer these questions. The answers are in the photo.

a) Becky wants to make a cup of tea. What does she need?
b) Sue wants to write a letter. What does she need?
c) Becky and Sarah want to wake up early. What do they need?
d) You want to buy a new pullover. What do you need?

5 SOUNDS   Showing surprise or interest

Listen to the cassette and repeat these phrases expressing surprise:

Really? / are you? / hasn't he?

Now listen again and repeat these phrases expressing no interest:

Really / are you? / hasn't he?

Now listen to these short conversations.
Does the second speaker show surprise or not? Put ticks:

	1	2	3	4	5	6
Surprise						
No surprise						

TRANSFER

1 ROLE PLAY
With your partner, write a list of Do's and Don'ts for your college or office.

OFFICE RULES

Do's	Don'ts
1	
2	
3	
4	
5	

It is your first day at your college or office. Ask your partner what you must and mustn't do.

2 READING
Five years ago only businessmen and women or very rich people had a computer. Now they are much cheaper and everyone can have one. This computer costs £130.
So yesterday you bought a computer and you want to do something with it. First, you must make it work, and it can't work alone. You need a TV and also a cassette recorder.
This is what you do. Connect the computer to the TV, with the white cable. Then connect the cassette recorder to the computer, with the black and red cable. Plug them into the back of the computer. Now switch on the TV and the cassette recorder. Now your computer is working, and you can start to write programmes, or play games. Good luck!

Find out what six instructions you must follow to make your computer work.

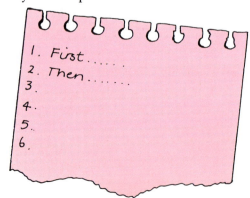

1. First ......
2. Then ......
3.
4.
5.
6.

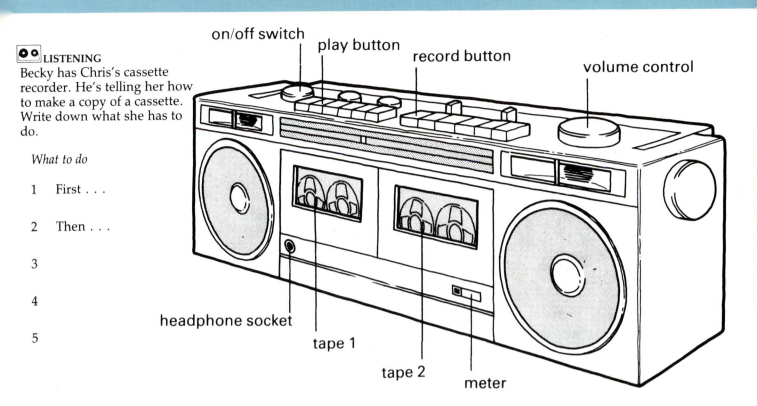

LISTENING

Becky has Chris's cassette recorder. He's telling her how to make a copy of a cassette. Write down what she has to do.

What to do

1 First . . .

2 Then . . .

3

4

5

on/off switch
play button
record button
volume control
headphone socket
tape 1
tape 2
meter

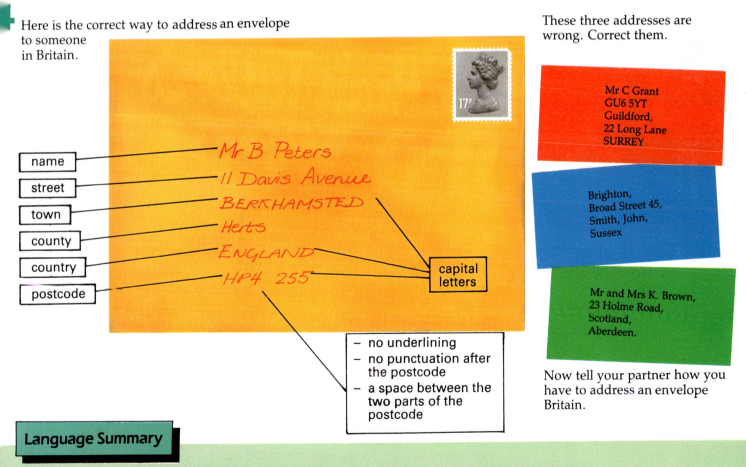

Here is the correct way to address an envelope to someone in Britain.

name — Mr B Peters
street — 11 Davis Avenue
town — BERKHAMSTED
county — Herts
country — ENGLAND
postcode — HP4 2SS

17P

capital letters

– no underlining
– no punctuation after the postcode
– a space between the two parts of the postcode

These three addresses are wrong. Correct them.

Mr C Grant
GU6 5YT
Guildford,
22 Long Lane
SURREY

Brighton,
Broad Street 45,
Smith, John,
Sussex

Mr and Mrs K. Brown,
23 Holme Road,
Scotland,
Aberdeen.

Now tell your partner how you have to address an envelope Britain.

Language Summary

Now you know how to:

● **Give instructions:**
Switch on the cassette recorder.
You must connect the computer to the TV.
Don't drive too fast.
You mustn't brake too hard.

● **Say what you need:**
You need a TV and also a cassette player.

Martin	48670.
Roger	Hello, Martin?
Martin	Yes, speaking.
Roger	This is Roger.
Martin	Oh, hello.
Roger	Listen, I have a problem.
Martin	Yes.
Roger	Somebody bought me a video cassette for my birthday, but I haven't got a video recorder. Can I borrow yours for a couple of days?
Martin	Yes, of course you can. When do you want to use i
Roger	Is it all right if I come over tonight?
Martin	No, I'm afraid we're going out. How about tomorrow evening?
Roger	That's great. Thanks. See you then. Bye.
Martin	Bye.

Check!

1 Who's got a video recorder?
2 When is Roger going to Martin's house?
3 Why is Roger going to Martin's house?

Jonathan Tatler's VIDEO WORLD

KNITTED DRESS,

Here are this week's new releases from the world of video. I worked very hard yesterday, and watched all of them in one evening – not a very good idea! So, what are they like? Wonderful, or rubbish like so many of the new videos this year?

First, *Skiing for Beginners*. I watched this very closely, because I can't ski, and I'd like to learn. The producers explained the instructions very well, and the instructors skied beautifully down the mountains, but I was still frightened. But, if you enjoy watching people ski and you want to learn, buy the video.

Now, videos from the world of television. Whose idea was it to take TV programmes and sell them on videocassette? I don't think it's a good idea. I prefer to see good films from the cinema. But some people like seeing the same comedy programme 23 times!

Skiing for Beginners

Check!

1 What does Jonathan Tatler do?
2 What did he do yesterday?

Asking for and giving opinions:	What are they like? / What's it like?	They're terrible. / It's wonderful.

I don't	enjoy / like	watching	old comedy programmes.
Some people prefer to watch			

Asking for, giving and refusing permission:	Is it all right if I / Can I	borrow your video?	Yes, of course you can. / No, I'm afraid you can't.

Adjectives and adverbs:	The skiing was beautiful. / The explanations were good.	He skied beautifully. / They explained things well.

Possessives:	Whose	idea was it? / video is it?	It	was / is	mine / yours / his / hers / ours / theirs

PRACTICE

1

A I went to the Rod Stewart concert last night.
B Oh, what was it like?
A It was all right, but not fantastic.
B I don't like going to concerts. I prefer to buy the LP.

Now you.
Make conversations like this, using these ideas:

STUDENT A

the Rolling Stones concert — very good
the new James Bond film — wonderful
Shakespeare's *Hamlet* — difficult to understand
the circus — terrible

STUDENT B

buy the LP
watch the video
read plays
watch sport

2 You are talking to your boss

A Is it all right if I / Can I come in late tomorrow?
B I'm afraid you can't. We've got a lot of work to do.

Ask permission for these things:
a) come in late tomorrow
b) take tomorrow morning off
c) have two hours for lunch
d) go on holiday next week
e) leave early this evening
Your partner can refuse or give permission

3 Ask your partner about a film, play or musical he or she saw.

A What was it like?
B It was quite good. They acted well and spoke slowly, so it was easy to understand. I enjoyed it.

act	move	good	marvellous
speak	talk	bad	boring
sing	dance	poor	slow

4 You want to borrow some of these things. Ask whose they are, and if you can borrow them.

A Whose is the calculator?
B It's mine.
A Can I borrow it for a minute?
B Of course. Take it?

a newspaper   Sellotape

a typewriter   a pen

a rubber

a pencil   a lighter   a calculator

5 SOUNDS   Lists

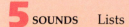 Listen to the cassette and repeat this complete list:

There's beer, wine, brandy, lager.

Now listen again and repeat this unfinished list:

There's beer, wine, brandy, lager . . .

Now listen to the cassette. Are these lists complete or unfinished? Put ticks:

	1	2	3	4	5	6
Complete						
Unfinished						

TRANSFER

1 You want to borrow some things from your partner, but you must give a good reason. Your partner must ask why you want something.

2 Talk to your partner about a concert or sporting event you went to, like this:
Liverpool played well. The goalkeeper was brilliant.
The orchestra was wonderful, and the singing was fantastic.

3 ROLE PLAY

You and your partners live in a house like 7 Royal Terrace. The house needs some repairs and you want to change some things about the house.

Make a list of repairs and changes.
One of your partners is the owner of the house.
Talk to him or her about your problems and ideas.

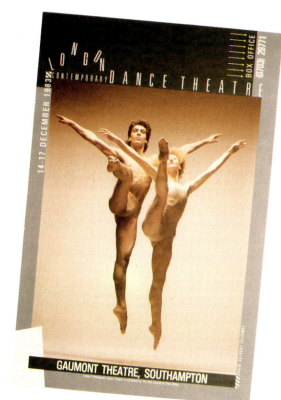

LISTENING

Two people are talking about a film they saw yesterday. What did they think of it?
Right or wrong (√ or ×)

Nick thought:

1 The film was very good. ☐
2 The special effects were bad. ☐
3 Natassia Kinski acted well. ☐

Jane thought:

1 The ending was good. ☐
2 The film was very exciting. ☐
3 The story was interesting. ☐

---

5 WRITING

Write a report on a film, play, concert, ballet performance or other event you saw recently.
Say what was good or bad about it.

Language Summary

Now you know how to:

- **Talk about opinions:**
  What was it like?   *It was terrible.*
  I don't enjoy watching TV. I prefer to go out.

- **Ask for and give or refuse permission:**
  Is it all right if I take a photo?   *No, I'm afraid you can't.*
  Can I borrow your pen?   *Yes, of course you can.*

- **Use adverbs:**
  He sang badly, but played the guitar well.

- **Use whose and possessives:**
  Whose is it?   *It's hers.*

Simon Wright, the chairman of the meeting	This morning we're going to talk about the new Head Office idea. We must discuss it ourselves first and then talk to the staff. Can I have your opinions, please?
Barry English	Well, I think we certainly need a new Head Office.
Simon	We all agree on that, Barry. But you must ask yourselves the question: where and when do we want to move?
Roger Eastwood	I think an office outside London is a good idea.
Claire Chambers	I agree.
Anne Levin	So do I. This office is expensive, and it isn't very convenient for our staff or customers.
Barry	I don't agree with you, Anne. The other big architect firms have their offices here. The banks are here too. And London is convenient for our customers from other countries.
Simon	That's true. But I agree with Anne. London isn't cheap. Croydon and Harlow, for example, are cheaper. What do you think of those places?
Roger	Harlow is a good idea. It's on the motorway now, so it's convenient for London and the new airport at Stansted. But I don't want to work in Croydon.
Claire	Neither do I. It's very near London, and it's still expensive.

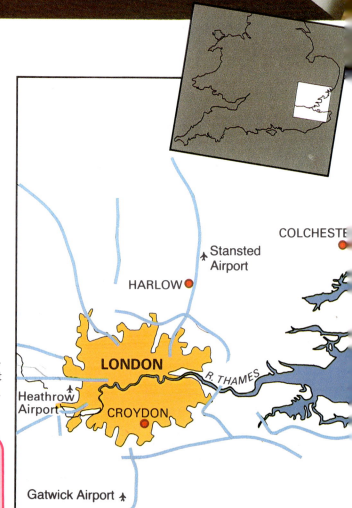

COLCHESTE
Stansted Airport
HARLOW
LONDON
R. THAMES
Heathrow Airport
CROYDON
Gatwick Airport

Check!

1 How many people want to move the office out of London?
2 Who does not want to move the office?
3 Why do people want to move the office?
4 Where does Roger want to move to and why is it a good choice?

Agreeing with someone:

A	B
I think an office outside London is a good idea.	I agree (with you). So do I.
I don't want to work in Croydon.	Neither do I.
London is convenient.	That's true.

Disagreeing with someone:

A	B
The London office isn't convenient for us. Harlow is very cheap.	I don't agree (with you). That isn't true!

Reflexive pronouns:

We must discuss it ourselves. You must ask yourselves the question.	I	myself	she	herself
	you	yourself	it	itself
		yourselves	we	ourselves
	he	himself	they	themselves

PRACTICE

1
Roger, Sue, David and Becky agreed or disagreed with these eight statements.
Talk to your partners, like this:

A   What do you think about London, Roger?

Roger   I think it's too busy and noisy. What do you think, Becky?

Becky   I disagree with you. I think . . . *ungusmanale*

2
What do you think of these eight statements? Do you agree or disagree with them? Discuss them with your partner.

3
WRITING
Write about the four people's opinions, like this:

Petrol is too expensive. Everyone agrees with that.

Motorists drive too fast on motorways. Sue, David and Roger agree with that, but Becky doesn't.

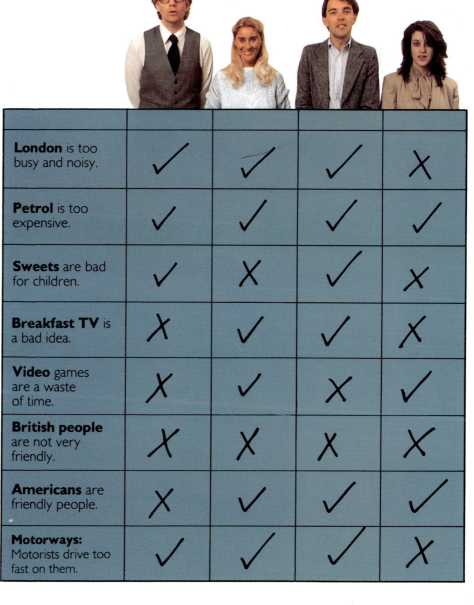

London is too busy and noisy.	✓	✓	✓	✗
Petrol is too expensive.	✓	✓	✓	✓
Sweets are bad for children.	✓	✗	✓	✗
Breakfast TV is a bad idea.	✗	✓	✓	✗
Video games are a waste of time.	✗	✓	✗	✓
British people are not very friendly.	✗	✗	✗	✗
Americans are friendly people.	✗	✓	✓	✓
Motorways: Motorists drive too fast on them.	✓	✓	✓	✗

4 SOUNDS Stress

Listen to the cassette and repeat these words with the stress at the beginning:

cústomers / árchitect / ínterviewer

Listen again and repeat these words with the stress later in the word:

internátional / conversátion / fantástic

Now listen to the cassette. Is the stress on the words at the beginning or later in the word? Put ticks:

	1	2	3	4	5	6	7	8
Beginning								
Later								

TRANSFER

1 DISCUSSION
Young people today.
Find out what your partners think about these statements.

They listen to terrible music.

Young people spend too much time at school and college.

They think only about themselves.

They watch too much television.

They don't work hard enough.

They get married too early.

2 WRITING
Write a short report about the opinions of the people in your group.

3 DISCUSSION

With your partner, discuss the topic: **Young people get married too early**
Here are some ideas –

★ 'When people are young, they don't understand what marriage means.'

★ 'It's good to be free until you are about 30. You can do everything you want before you get married.'

★ 'Women want to have a career before they have children.'

★ 'Early marriages often break up.'

★ 'People know what they're doing even when they are young.'

★ 'You can be married *and* free. Young married couples can do everything they want *together*.'

★ 'Women can have their children early and then start their jobs.'

★ 'All kinds of marriages break up.'

• What is a good age to get married?

• Why is this a good age?

• What makes a good marriage?

4 LISTENING

Here are seven sentences about the conversation between Mike, Carol and Brian.

Which four statements are wrong and which three right. Put a √ or ✗

1 There are 500 empty houses in Colchester. ☐
2 The empty houses have all got broken doors and windows. ☐
3 Nobody wants to buy the empty houses. ☐
4 There are 400 families with no homes. ☐
5 These families do not want to live in the empty houses. ☐
6 Last year the police moved some families out of the empty houses. ☐
7 Carol thinks people must pay to live in the empty houses. ☐

Language Summary

Now you know how to:

• **Give your opinion:**

   I think London is very convenient.

• **Agree with someone:**

   I think it's a bad idea.   *I agree with you. So do I.*

   I don't think it's a good idea.   *Neither do I.*

• **Disagree with someone:**

   I think it's expensive.   *I don't agree with you. That isn't true.*

• **Use reflexive pronouns:**

   We must discuss it ourselves.

At 7 in the morning, on April 12th 1981, the first Space Shuttle left Earth. It flew up into space at a speed of 28,000 kilometres per hour, with two astronauts inside. The first men to fly *Columbia* were John W. Young and Robert L. Crippen. They worked hard in space – they took photographs, sent TV pictures back to Earth, and tested *Columbia's* controls.

After two days in space, *Columbia* came back to Earth, the first American spaceship to land like a plane and not in the sea, and at 13.21 it stopped safely at Rogers Air Base in the Californian desert. *Columbia* was a great success. It showed the world that it was possible to send a spaceship into space, bring it back like an aeroplane and send it up again.

That was the beginning of the Space Shuttle's work. In 1983, the ship *Challenger* made its first flight, and now there are four Shuttles – *Columbia, Challenger, Discovery* and *Atlantis*. They can do a lot of useful work: they can take satellites into space, and they can also bring them back for repair. They can help scientists do special experiments, take pictures of the stars, and learn more about the Earth's weather. At the moment, only astronauts, scientists and engineers can fly in the Shuttle, but soon ordinary people are going to have a chance to buy a ticket on the Shuttle – to space and back.

Check!

1   When did the first Shuttle leave Earth?
2   Where did *Columbia* land?
3   Who were the astronauts on *Columbia*?
4   What did the astronauts do when they were in space?
5   What other work can the Shuttle do?
6   Who is going to fly on the Shuttle in future?
7   How is the Shuttle different from other spaceships?
8   When did *Challenger* first fly?

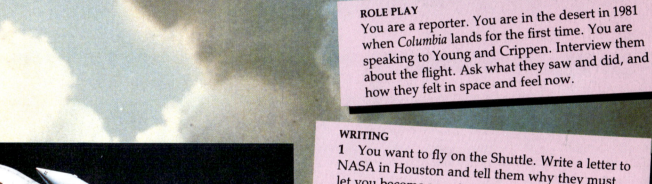

Shuttle statistics
The Shuttle is 37 metres long, 17 metres high and 24 metres wide. When it takes off it weighs 2,000,000 kilograms, because of the big rocket. When it lands it only weighs 85,000 kilograms.

It can fly at 28,000 kilometres per hour in space, and when it lands it is faster than a normal plane – it lands at 345 kilometres per hour.

The Shuttle can take seven people into space, and can carry ten people in an emergency.

It can carry satellites or other equipment into space – up to 29,000 kilograms of extra equipment, satellites or experiments. When it cornes back to Earth, the temperature on the outside is 2000°C.

ROLE PLAY

You and your friends want to go on holiday together next summer. Here are some of the holiday advertisements you are looking at.

Discuss the good and bad things about each of these holidays and decide which place you will *all* go to.

You can talk about:

- the weather
- the food
- the people
- the language
- the sights
- the places to go to
- the sport facilities
- the special trips
- the nightlife

Decide where you want to go to and why.

There's always something to see in

GREECE

THAILAND

Sun in the morning
Sights in the afternoon

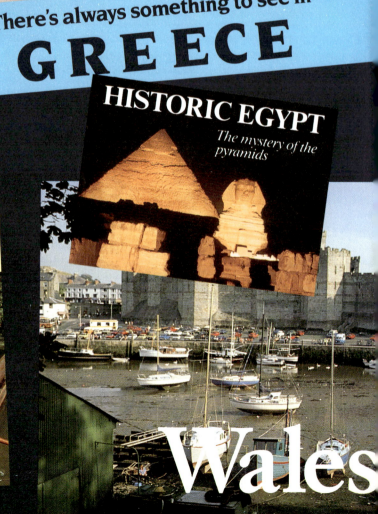

HISTORIC EGYPT

The mystery of the pyramids

Wales

This year forget the sea
Go on Safari in

Kenya

Come to sunny **SPAIN**

R · O · M · E

St Peters   The Colosseum   Delicious food & wine

You want a place with sea, sand, swimming and windsurfing.

You want a place with museums and sights to visit.

You want a place with a lot of sports facilities and activities.

You want a place where you can tour. You like walking in beautiful countryside and fishing.

You want a place with swimming, sun, and old things to see.

You want a place with sun, discos, young people and sailing.

las everything – sun, sea,
and, history and culture,
akes and mountains

Vocabulary

The number beside each word shows the unit in which the word first appears.

A

a bit 22
a, an 1
ache 27
act (vb) 28
activity 30
address 1
advertisement 12
after 8
afternoon 13
age 29
agree 29
air 27
air stewardess 8
air traffic controller 8
airport 5
alarm 27
alarm clock 27
alcohol 14
all 7
all right 11
along 10
also 14
always 7
and 1
angry 20
another 25
any 11
anybody 20
anyway 15
apple 11
appoint 20
appointment 11
April 18
architect 1
are 2
aren't 3
around 15
arrival 8
arrive 5
ask 7
astronaut 30
at 3
at home 3
at the moment 11
attic 5
aubergine 17
August 18
avenue 10
away 24

B

back 13
bacon 14
bad 24
bad 12
badminton 14
banana 11
bank 15
bank manager 11
bar 8
bargain 12
baseball 21
basement 3
bath 4
bathroom 4
battery 12
beach 14
beautiful 9
because 8
bed 7
bedroom 4
beer 21
before 20
beginning 30
behind 10
best 23
better 15
between 10

big 6
bird 19
birthday 21
biscuits 14
black 12
blue 12
boat 15
boatyard 15
body 21
bomb 22
book 15
book (vb) 18
bookshop 5
bored 20
born 23
borrow 28
boss 11
bowl 4
boy 16
box 17
brake 27
bread 14
break 15
break up 29
breakfast 14
bridge 5
bring 25
British 12
brochure 11
broken 29
brother 9
brown 12
build 16
building 19
burn 23
bus station 5
businessman 14
busy 3
but 13
butter 17
button 27
buy 15
bypass 10

C

cable 27
café 5
cake 14
calculator 28
call (vb) 24
camera 9
cameraman 16
camping 26
can 7
can't 26
canteen 10
car 4
car park 10
carrots 14
cassette 1
cassette recorder 27
central 6
centre 5
certainly 10
chair 4
change 16
cheap 9
check 27
check-in desk 8
cheese 14
chess 26
child 7
children 7
chocolate 14
choice 29
church 15
cigarette 17
cinema 6
city 11
class 1

close 5
clothes 12
club 5
code 16
coffee 7
college 10
comb 7
come back 18
come in 1
come on 12
come over 28
comedy 7
comfortable 9
company 6
competition 26
computer 8
concert 22
connect 27
contract 6
convenient 29
cooker 4
copy 27
correctly 27
corridor 10
cost 16
costume 16
could 25
country 14
countryside 21
county 27
couple 29
cousin 6
cover 27
crash 23
crazy 22
crowd 13
cup 4
cupboard 4
customer 29

D

dark 12
day 8
December 18
decorating 26
delicious 30
dentist 11
department 25
departure 8
depend 20
desert 30
designer 1
desk 8
destination 11
diary 18
die 23
diet 14
different 6
difficult 20
dining room 4
dinner 21
director 24
disagree 29
disappear 21
disco 5
discuss 14
do 1
doctor 2
documentary 7
does 3
door 4
double 11
downstairs 4
draw 26
drink 7
driver 17
dynamic 24

E

each 12

earlier 24
early 29
easy 8
eat 14
editor 14
egg 17
eight 1
eighteen 2
eighty 7
electric 9
electricity 27
eleven 2
else 24
empty 29
end 10
energy 20
engine 4
engineer 2
enjoy 15
enough 17
equipment 27
especially 7
estate agent 16
evening 6
every 8
everybody 20
everyone 13
excuse me 1
exercise 20
exit 26
expensive 9
experiment 30
explain 28
extra 24

F

face 13
facilities 30
factory 5
family 6
famous 13
fancy 15
fantastic 12
fare 16
farmer 22
fast 9
fat 19
father 11
February 18
fed up 20
feel 27
ferry 16
field 21
fifteen 2
fifty 7
fill in 24
film 6
filmstar 3
find 10
fine 2
finish 14
fire 13
firm 29
first 10
fish 14
five 1
flat 3
flight 11
flour 17
fly (vb) 18
food 7
football 6
football match 28
for 5
forest 21
forget 27
fork 4
form 1
fortune 27
forty 7

four 1
fourteen 2
fourth 18
free 11
free time 6
freezer 4
Friday 7
fridge 4
friend 15
friendly 16
frightened 28
fun 15
furniture 24
fuse 27

G

garage 25
get 14
get married 22
get up 8
gift 8
girl 16
give 8
glad 21
glass 17
golf 14
go off 22
go out 28
good 6
good afternoon 1
good evening 1
good morning 1
goodbye 1
got 7
government 26
grade 27
grapefruit 11
great 4
green 12
greengrocer 5
group 14
guide 5
guitar 26
gun 23

H

hair 13
hairdresser 11
half 11
half past 11
hall 4
hamburgers 7
happen 22
happy 20
hard 15
has 4
hat 9
hate 7
have 4
have got 9
have got to 24
have to 24
he 3
head office 29
headlight 4
headphones 27
healthy 20
heating 27
heavy 19
height 19
hello 1
help 7
her 9
here 1
here's 5
hers 28
herself 29
hey 9
high 19
him 11

117

Infinitive	Past tense	Present tense he/she/it	verb + ing
be	was, were	is	being
become	became	becomes	becom...
begin	began	begins	begin...
break	broke	breaks	break...
bring	brought	brings	bring...
build	built	builds	build...
buy	bought	buys	buyin...
can	could	can	
catch	caught	catches	catch...
choose	chose	chooses	choos...
come	came	comes	comin...
cost	cost	costs	costin...
cut	cut	cuts	cuttin...
do	did	does	doing
draw	drew	draws	draw...
drink	drank	drinks	drinki...
drive	drove	drives	drivin...
eat	ate	eats	eating
fall	fell	falls	falling
feel	felt	feels	feelin...
find	found	finds	findin...
fly	flew	flies	flying
forget	forgot	forgets	forget...
get	got	gets	gettin...
give	gave	gives	giving
go	went	goes	going
grow	grew	grows	growi...
have	had	has	having
hear	heard	hears	hearin...
hit	hit	hits	hitting
hold	held	holds	holdir...
hurt	hurt	hurts	hurtin...
keep	kept	keeps	keepin...
know	knew	knows	knowi...
learn	learnt	learns	learnin...
leave	left	leaves	leavin...
lend	lent	lends	lendin...
let	let	lets	letting
lie	lay	lies	lying
lose	lost	loses	losing
make	made	makes	makin...
meet	met	meets	meetin...
pay	paid	pays	paying
put	put	puts	puttin...
read	read	reads	readin...
ride	rode	rides	riding
ring	rang	rings	ringin...
run	ran	runs	runnin...
say	said	says	saying
see	saw	sees	seeing
sell	sold	sells	selling
send	sent	sends	sendir...
show	showed	shows	showi...
shut	shut	shuts	shuttir...
sing	sang	sings	singin...
sit	sat	sits	sitting
sleep	slept	sleeps	sleepir...
speak	spoke	speaks	speaki...
spell	spelt	spells	spellin...
spend	spent	spends	spendi...
take	took	takes	taking
teach	taught	teaches	teachir...
tell	told	tells	telling
think	thought	thinks	thinkir...
throw	threw	throws	throwi...
wake up	woke up	wakes up	waking
wear	wore	wears	wearin...
win	won	wins	winnin...
write	wrote	writes	writing

Drills

Unit 1

Drill 1 *example:* Sue Eastwood/a designer
Hello, I'm Sue Eastwood. I'm a designer.

1 Sue Eastwood/a designer
2 Mark Taylor/a student
3 Roger Eastwood/an architect
4 Ellen Taylor/a secretary
5 Patrick Jones/a student

Drill 2 *example:* What's your name? (Sue)
My name's Sue.
What do you do? (designer)
I'm a designer.

1 What's your name? (Sue)
2 What do you do? (designer)
3 What's your name? (Mark)
4 What do you do? (student)
5 What's your name? (Ellen)

Drill 3 Listen and repeat these numbers:

a seven-four-six-five-two.
b eight-nine-one-three-six
c three-five-nine-one-nine-seven
d nine-nine-nine

Unit 2

Drill 1 *example:* Mark/Ellen/Los Angeles
Hello. I'm Mark and this is Ellen. We're from Los Angeles.

1 Mark/Ellen/Los Angeles
2 Sue/Roger/Colchester
3 Sarah/Chris/England
4 Ellen/Mark/America
5 David/John/London

Drill 2 *example:* Hello, I'm Chris.
Hello Chris. Where are you from?

1 Hello, I'm Chris.
2 Hello, I'm Ellen.
3 Hello, I'm Sue.
4 Hello, I'm Roger.

Drill 3 *example:* –13–
twelve thirteen fourteen

a –13–   c –12–   e –18–
b –19–   d –17–   f –14–

Unit 3

Drill 1 *example:* Is Sue a designer? (yes)
Yes, she is.
Are Mark and Ellen from England? (no)
No, they aren't.

1 Is Roger a teacher? (no)
2 Are Roger and Sue from America? (no)
3 Is Ellen a secretary? (yes)
4 Is Mark a student? (yes)
5 Are you from England? (no)

Drill 2 *example:* Roger/designer
Is Roger a designer?
Ellen/America
Is Ellen from America?

1 Mark/student
2 Roger and Sue/Colchester
3 Mrs Brown/secretary
4 Alan/Brighton
5 Jenny and Mary/at home

Drill 3 *example:* Sarah
What does Sarah do?

1 Sarah
2 Roger
3 Mark and John
4 they
5 Jake and Sarah

Drill 4 *example:* What does Roger do? (an architect)
He's an architect.

1 What does Roger do? (an architect)
2 What does Sue do? (a designer)
3 What does Mark do? (a student)
4 What do Mark and John do? (students)
5 What do David and Mary do? (teachers)

Unit 4

Drill 1 *example:* What's this? (fridge)
It's a fridge.
example: Where's the fridge? (kitchen)
It's in the kitchen.

1 What's this? (fridge)
2 Where's the fridge? (kitchen)
3 What's this? (television)
4 Where's the television? (bedroom)
5 What's this? (freezer)

Drill 2 Look at the map on page 15.
example: Where's the cinema?
It's in Albion Road.

1 Where's the museum?
2 Where's the supermarket?
3 Where's the sports centre?
4 Where's the theatre?

Drill 3 *example:* kitchen/fridge and freezer
The kitchen has a fridge and a freezer.

1 kitchen/fridge and freezer
2 John's room/sofa and three chairs
3 living-room/video and a television
4 dining-room/table and four chairs

Unit 5

Drill 1 *example:* Is there a sports centre? (yes)
Yes, there is
Is there a theatre? (no)
No, there isn't.

1 Is there a sports centre? (yes)
2 Is there a theatre? (no)
3 Is there a bookshop? (no)
4 Is there a shopping centre? (yes)
5 Is there a train at 10 o'clock? (yes)

Drill 2 *example:* The bank opens at 10 o'clock.
When does it open?

1 The museum opens at 5 o'clock.
2 The London train leaves at 2 o'clock.
3 The school closes at 4 o'clock.
4 The bus arrives at 9 o'clock.
5 The shop opens at 8 o'clock.

Drill 3

Colchester	6 o'clock → London
Colchester	7 o'clock → Clacton
Colchester	8 o'clock → Cambridge
Colchester	9 o'clock → Norwich

example: Is this the train for London?
             Yes it is. It leaves at six o'clock.

1 Is this the train for London?
2 Is this the train for Clacton?
3 Is this the train for Cambridge?
4 Is this the train for Norwich?

Unit 6

Drill 1 *example:*   I work in London. (Mary/Colchester)
                  Mary works in Colchester.

1 I work in London. (John/Manchester)
2 I come from America. (Peter/England)
3 Jane lives in London. (Mike and Janet/Birmingham)
4 Sue plays tennis. (Becky/squash)
5 We go to the cinema in the evening. (Mary/theatre)

Drill 2 *example:*   Michael goes to London at the weekend.
                  When does he go to London?

1 Michael goes to London at the weekend.
2 Sue goes to the theatre in the evening.
3 Mark and Ellen come home at 6 o'clock.
4 John goes to the sports centre at the weekend.
5 Ellen goes to work at 8 o'clock.

Drill 3 *example:*   What sport does Sue play? (tennis)
                  She plays tennis.

1 What sport does Mark play? (football)
2 And John? (table tennis)
3 And what about Roger? (tennis)
4 And Becky? (squash)

Unit 7

Drill 1 *example:*   Does Roger like sports programmes? (yes)
                  Yes, he does.
                  Does Sue watch TV? (no)
                  No, she doesn't.

1 Does he like sports programmes? (yes)
2 Does she watch the nine o'clock news? (no)
3 Do they go to bed at eight o'clock? (yes)
4 Does she like football? (no)
5 Do your children watch TV on Saturday morning? (yes)

Drill 2 *example:*   Roger likes television. (the nine o'clock
                  news?)
                  Does he watch the nine o'clock news?

1 Sue likes television. (sports programmes?)
2 Mark and John like television. (news programmes?)
3 Sarah likes television. (children's programmes?)
4 Chris likes television. (the late film?)

Drill 3 *example:*   Jim/Monday
                  What does Jim do on Monday?

1 Jim/Monday
2 Sarah/Tuesday
3 Paul/Friday
4 Sarah and Sue/Saturday
5 Sue and Roger/Saturday

Unit 9

Drill 1 *example:*   I/new car.
                  I've got a new car.

1 I/new car.
2 Peter/old car.
3 they/small house.
4 she/good job.
5 I/expensive watch.

Drill 2 *example:*   Has Roger got a big car? (small)
                  No he hasn't. He's got a small car.

1 Has Roger got a big car? (small)
2 Has Sue got a small house? (big)
3 Has Mary got an expensive camera? (cheap)
4 Has Michael got a big flat? (small)

Drill 3 *example:*   My car is very old. (new)
                  I want a new car.

1 My car is very old. (new)
2 Mark and Ellen's car is very old. (new)
3 Her car is very old. (new)
4 Our car is very slow. (fast)
5 Their car is very slow. (fast)

Unit 10

Drill 1 *example:*   The George Hotel
                  Excuse me. Can you tell me where the
                  George Hotel is, please?

1 The George Hotel
2 Nunns Road
3 The High Street
4 The station
5 The bus station

Drill 2 *example:*   Where's my coat? (in the bedroom)
                  It's in the bedroom.

1 Where's the car? (car park)
2 Where are my new books? (John's flat)
3 Where are Mark and Ellen? (sitting room)
4 Where's my new camera? (bedroom)
5 Where's my coat? (bedroom)

Drill 3 Look at the map of Washington on page 37.
      example: Where's the Capitol?
                  It's near Constitution Avenue.

1 Where's the White House?
2 Where's the station?
3 Where's the Washington Monument?
4 Where's the Smithsonian Institute?

Unit 11

Drill 1 *example:*   Can I help you? (hotels in London)
                  Yes. I'd like some information about hotels
                  in London, please.

1 Can I help you? (trains to Cambridge)
2 Can I help you? (flights to Madrid)
3 Can I help you? (hotels in Manchester)
4 Can I help you? (cinemas in London)

Drill 2 *example:*   postcards (yes)
                  We've got some postcards.
                  theatre tickets (no)
                  We haven't got any theatre tickets.

1 postcards (yes)
2 brochures (yes)
3 English apples (no)
4 stamps (no)
5 maps of England (yes)

Drill 3 *example:*   brochures
                     Have you got any brochures?

1 brochures about Spain
2 addresses of cheap hotels
3 tickets for the theatre tonight
4 information about Mexico City

Unit 12

Drill 1 *example:*   that red jacket?
                     How much is that red jacket?
                     those black jeans?
                     How much are those black jeans?

1 that red jacket?
2 those black jeans?
3 that car stereo?
4 those blank cassettes?
5 that white shirt?

Drill 2 *example:*   cassette
                     How many cassettes would you like?

1 cassettes
2 batteries
3 shirts
4 pullovers
5 pens

Drill 3 *example:*   green jacket/blue
                     I don't want a green jacket. Have you got a
                     blue one?

1 green jacket/blue
2 black pullover/red
3 red shirt/white
4 expensive radio/cheap
5 old pullover/new

Unit 13

Drill 1 *example:*   Where's Peter? (talking to Sue)
                     He's talking to Sue.

1 Where's Margaret? (watching TV)
2 Where are Chris and Mark? (shopping)
3 Where's Simon? (reading the newspaper)
4 Where are Paul and Jenny? (having lunch)

Drill 2 *example:*   John's talking
                     Who's he talking to?

1 John's talking.
2 Chris is writing a letter.
3 Ellen's talking on the 'phone.
4 Roger's writing a postcard.

Drill 3 *example:*   10.10
                     It's ten past ten

a 10.10
b   8.15
c 11.50
d   6.35
e   5.20

Unit 14

Drill 1 *example:*   Mr Jefferson/teaching
                     Mr Jefferson isn't teaching today.

1 Mr Jefferson/teaching
2 Mrs Jackson/teaching
3 Peter and Jane/working
4 Mr Chambers/playing tennis
5 Roger/working in London

Drill 2 *example:*   I work in London. (Colchester)
                     But I'm not working in London today. I'm
                     working in Colchester.

1 He works in London. (Oxford)
2 She works in London. (Liverpool)
3 Roger works in London. (Cambridge)
4 The MP works in London. (Colchester)
5 They work in London. (Dover)

Drill 3 *example:*   Sarah works in Colchester.
                     Is she working in Colchester at the
                     moment?

1 Sarah works in Colchester.
2 She meets people.
3 The MP writes letters.
4 They talk to businessmen.
5 Mark lives in Los Angeles.

Unit 15

Drill 1 *example:*   go to the cinema in the evening (yes)
                     I usually go to the cinema in the evening.
                     go on holiday in winter (no)
                     I don't usually go on holiday in winter.

1 meet my friends at the weekend (yes)
2 go to work at eight o'clock (yes)
3 work on Saturday and Sunday (no)
4 read the newspaper at work (no)
5 go to London at the weekend (yes)

Drill 2 *example:*   I usually work in London . . . (go on
                     holiday this week)
                     but I'm going on holiday this week

1 He usually works in Parliament . . . (Colchester today)
2 We usually take the bus to work . . . (walking this week)
3 Roger usually has a sandwich for lunch . . . (roast beef
   today)
4 Mr and Mrs Stewart usually go to Blackpool on holiday
   . . . (Spain this year)
5 Peter usually works in London . . . (Oxford today)

Unit 17

Drill 1 *example:*   Have you got enough time? (yes)
                     Yes, I've got plenty of time
                     Have you got enough money? (no)
                     No, I haven't got any money

1 Have you got enough English money? (yes)
2 Has Mark got enough presents? (yes)
3 Have Chris and Jane got any postcards? (no)
4 Have we got enough coffee? (no)

Drill 2 *examples:*   money
                      They haven't got **much** money.
                      postcards
                      They haven't got **many** postcards.

1 money
2 postcards
3 time
4 souvenirs of London
5 American money

Drill 3 *example:*   We haven't got much money . . . (friends)
                     but we've got a lot of friends

1 John hasn't got much English money . . . (French
   money)
2 Ellen hasn't got many souvenirs . . . (photographs)
3 They haven't got much time this morning . . . (this
   afternoon)
4 I haven't got many photos of London . . . (Edinburgh)

Unit 18

Drill 1 *example:* Anne Green/fly/Monday
    Anne Green's going to fly on Monday.

1 John and Philip/arrive/tomorrow
2 Anne/come back/Friday
3 David/leave/next week
4 Alan/work late/tonight

Drill 2 *example:* Is Roger going to fly from Gatwick?
    (Heathrow)
    No, he isn't. He's going to fly from
    Heathrow.

1 Is he going to stay in San Francisco? (Washington)
2 Is he going to come back on Monday? (Saturday)
3 Is Sue going to go with him? (Edinburgh)
4 Is she going to stay with her mother? (sister)

Drill 3 *example:* Joan/October 6th
    Roger's going to see Joan on October **the
    sixth**.

1 Joan/October 6th
2 Mark/January 3rd
3 His mother/March 18th
4 Mr Gregory/April 20th

Unit 19

Drill 1 *example:* The George Hotel is as big as the Rossiya
    Hotel.
    No, it isn't! The Rossiya Hotel is bigger
    than the George Hotel.

1 The George Hotel is as big as the Rossiya Hotel.
2 The Golden Gate Bridge is as long as the Humber Bridge.
3 Roger Eastwood is as tall as Dan Busch.
4 British cars are as big as American cars.
5 British people are as friendly as American people.

Drill 2 *example:* Is Tokyo a big city?
    It certainly is. It's the biggest city in the
    world.

1 Is Chicago airport busy?
2 Is Dan Busch tall?
3 Is the Humber bridge long?
4 Is the Sahara Desert large?

Drill 3 *example:* France/big/Germany
    France is as big as Germany

1 France/big/Germany
2 John/tall/Sarah
3 A Mercedes/fast/A Ferrari
4 American food/good/British food
5 The Grand Hotel/expensive/The Hilton

Unit 20

Drill 1 *example:* When do you leave home in the morning?
    (usually/8 o'clock)
    I usually leave at 8 o'clock.

1 When do you arrive at work? (usually/9 o'clock)
2 When do you go to the cinema? (sometimes/Friday evening)
3 And when do you watch TV? (sometimes/in the evening)
4 And when do you play tennis? (usually/Sunday afternoon)

Drill 2 *example:* I often go to work by train. (car?)
    Do you ever go by car?

1 Roger often goes to Europe on business. (America?)
2 I often work in the evening. (Saturdays?)
3 I often see Peter at the shops. (Michael?)
4 We often go for a drink after work. (meal?)

Drill 3 *example:* Where was John yesterday? (London)
    He was in London.

1 Where was Mary yesterday? (Manchester)
2 Where were Geoff and Anne last week? (on holiday)
3 Where were you in August? (in France)
4 Where were you and your friends last night? (at John's house)

Unit 21

Drill 1 *example:* What did Roger do in Washington? (work
    hard)
    He worked hard.

1 What did Roger do in Washington? (ask a lot of questions)
2 What did he do in the office? (interview some people)
3 What did he do in the evening? (work hard)
4 What did he visit? (the White House and the Senate)

Drill 2 *example:* Did you see the sights? (the White House)
    Yes, I did. I saw the White House.

1 Did Roger see the sights? (the Capitol)
2 Did he go out in the evening? (the cinema)
3 Did he fly to America? (Washington)
4 Did he take any photos? (a lot)

Drill 3 *example:* Where did Peter go yesterday? (Paris)
    He went to Paris.

1 Which sights did Roger see in America? (The Space Museum) (The White House)
2 Who did Sue stay with in Aberdeen? (her sister)
3 What did Mark do last night? (play tennis)
4 What did Ellen and Cathy do yesterday? (go into town)

Unit 22

Drill 1 *example:* Did Geoff go to Scotland? (Wales)
    No, he didn't. He went to Wales.
    Did he stay in a hotel? (a tent)
    No, he didn't. He stayed in a tent.

1 Did Becky see a play last night? (film)
2 Did Becky speak to John? (Peter)
3 Did Paul and Alan think the play was good? (terrible)
4 Did they meet in London? (Nottingham)

Drill 2 *example:* Roger went to America (Washington?)
    Did he go to Washington?

1 Roger saw a lot of the sights. (the White House?)
2 Geoff stayed in Wales last weekend. (a hotel?)
3 He spoke to some farmers. (English?)
4 He left in the morning. (at 5 o'clock?)

Drill 3 *example:* Did you like the weather in England? (no,
    terrible)
    No, I didn't. I thought it was terrible.
    Did you like the food? (yes, great)
    Yes, I did. I thought it was great.

1 Did you like the weather in England? (no, terrible)
2 Did you like the food? (yes, great)
3 And did you like the people? (yes, fantastic)
4 Did you enjoy the flight to London? (no, too long)
5 Did you enjoy your holiday? (no, too expensive)

Unit 24

Drill 1 *example:* Can you come to lunch on Saturday? (go to a wedding)
I'm sorry, I can't. I have to go to a wedding on Saturday.

1 Can you come to the cinema on Friday? (go to the doctor)
2 Can you meet me tomorrow evening? (work late)
3 Can you have lunch with me on Monday? (go to London)
4 Can we have dinner tonight? (do some work)

Drill 2 *example:* I'm staying until Sunday.
Do you have to stay until Sunday?

1 I'm staying until Sunday.
2 I'm going to my cousin's wedding.
3 I'm working at the weekend.
4 I'm going away for the weekend.

Drill 3 *example:* I've got to work this weekend.
But you had to work last weekend.

1 I've got to help the boss this weekend.
2 I've got to repair the car this weekend.
3 I've got to do some extra work tonight.
4 I've got to speak at the Town Hall this weekend.

Unit 25

Drill 1 *example:* We could stop another car. (phone a garage)
I'm not keen on that idea. Let's phone a garage.

1 We could ask another driver for help. (phone your brother)
2 We could phone from that house. (find a phone box)
3 We could buy a van. (buy a car)
4 We could ask that man. (ask a policeman)

Drill 2 *example:* take you to the nearest garage?
Shall I take you to the nearest garage?

1 take you to the nearest garage?
2 take you to the garage in my van?
3 change the wheel for you?
4 call a garage for you?
5 take you to your hotel in my car?

Drill 3 *example:* go to the cinema
Why don't we go to the cinema?

1 go to the cinema
2 find a garage
3 phone your brother
4 stop another driver
5 change the wheel here

Unit 26

Drill 1 *example:* Would you like to go sailing on Sunday?
(yes) Yes, I'd love to.
(no) Sorry, I can't – but thanks anyway.

1 Would you like to go sailing on Sunday? (yes)
2 Would you like to go sailing on Saturday? (no)
3 Would you like to come up for the weekend? (yes)
4 Would you like to play tennis on Wednesday evening? (no)

Drill 2 *example:* Can you sail?
Yes, I can. I like sailing.

1 Can you sail?
2 Can you play tennis?
3 Can you swim?
4 Can you play football?

Drill 3 *example:* sailing
Would you like to go sailing with me?

1 go sailing
2 come to a party
3 have a drink
4 come on holiday
5 play tennis

Unit 27

Drill 1 *examples:* You must watch me.
Watch me!
You mustn't drive too fast.
Don't drive too fast!

1 You must watch me.
2 You mustn't drive too fast.
3 You must take the old fuse out.
4 You mustn't brake too hard.
5 You mustn't be late.

Drill 2 *examples:* Use this petrol (yes)
You must use this petrol
Brake too hard (no)
You mustn't brake too hard.

1 Drive too fast (no)
2 Be late (no)
3 Check the air in your tyres (yes)
4 Screw the cover back on the plug (yes)

Drill 3 *example:* Becky's TV isn't working. (some help)
She needs some help.

1 My radio isn't working. (some help)
2 They want to change the plug. (a screwdriver)
3 David's big car's using too much petrol. (a smaller car)
4 Your flat's very small. (a bigger flat)

Unit 28

Drill 1 *example:* I've got a new car
Really! What's it like?
I've got some new books.
Really! What are they like?

1 I've got a new pullover.
2 I've got some new jeans.
3 Jane's got two new records.
4 We've got a new computer in the office.
5 Mike's got a new jacket.

Drill 2 *example:* playing tennis/play golf
I don't like playing tennis; I prefer to play golf.

1 playing tennis/play golf
2 watching television/go to the cinema
3 driving/go by train
4 going to restaurants/eat at home
5 working in the morning/work at night

Drill 3 *example:* borrow your video recorder?
                    Is it all right if I borrow your video
                    recorder?

1 borrow your video recorder?
2 come late?
3 watch this film on your TV?
4 use your video cassette for a couple of days?
5 go out this evening?

Unit 29

Drill 1 *example:* I think it's a good idea
                    So do I.
                    I don't think it's a good idea.
                    Neither do I.

1 I think it's a good idea.
2 I don't think it's a good idea.
3 I think we need a new office.
4 I don't think an office outside London is a good idea.
5 I don't think it's expensive.

Drill 2 *example:* What do you think of Harlow (good
                    idea/convenient)
                    I think Harlow's a good idea. It's
                    convenient.

1 What do you think of Harlow? (good idea/convenient)
2 What do you think of Croydon? (bad idea/expensive)
3 What do you think of an office outside London? (good idea/cheaper)
4 What do you think of a new Head Office? (good idea/not convenient here)

Drill 3 Listen to these opinions.

I think English men are wonderful.
I don't agree. I think they're terrible.

1 British food is the best in the world.
2 Scotland's football team is fantastic.
3 English weather is marvellous.
4 English is a very easy language to learn.

Acknowledgements

The publishers would like to thank the following for permission to reproduce photographs, illustrations and texts:

Zomo Publicity; V.A.G. (UK); Volvo Concessionaires; N & G Insight; Fiat UK; Renault UK; Camera Press; Ford Motor Company; British Airports Authority; Watches of Switzerland; The George Hotel, Colchester; Cunard Line; Lovis Ross; Just Boats, Crick, Northamptonshire; Bwrdd Croesco Cymru/Wales Tourist Board; British Rail (Western Region); Aer Lingus; Sealink UK; Guinness Superlatives; Novost Press Agency; David Lee Photography; Swiss National Tourist Office; GLC; Gillette UK; Lyceum Ballroom; Wembley Stadium; Barbican Centre; Hammersmith Palais; National Portrait Gallery; Royal Shakespeare Company; Jarrold Colour Publications; Local Hero – an Enigma production for Goldcrest, distributed in the UK by Twentieth Century Fox; London Contemporary Dance Theatre; Tim Furniss; Phil Marshall; Spanish Tourist Office; National Tourist Organisation of Greece; Tourist Authority of Thailand; Egypt Tourist Information.

The publishers and authors would like to thank the following for their help in producing this book:

The Donna Maria Organisation; Ana Pilan Vigil; Harumi Watanabe; Kayoko Mochiziki; Mark Ravina; Lifestyle and Confectionary Departments, The Army and Navy, High St, Bromley; British Rail, Sevenoaks; The Job Centre, Sevenoaks; Sarah's Greengrocer, Dunton Green; The Dorset Arms, Sevenoaks; Mrs C. Fulford-Smith; Nicholas Perry; Oliver Perry; Sevenoaks Travel; G. Jupp; Mark Barratt; Eurocentre, Lee Green; Mike Cooper; Chapman and Hanson Chartered Architects; Paul Cressall; The Bookshop, Blackheath; Leo Perry.

Designed by Stephen Raw, Letterforms.

Illustrations by Simon Ainley, Paul Crompton,
Illustra Graphics, Martin Salisbury, Swanston Graphics.
Location and studio photography by Melvyn Gill.

Typeset by Rowland Phototypesetting Ltd in 10pt Palatino
Origination by Colorcraft Ltd, Hong Kong.

Printed in Hong Kong by Colorcraft Ltd
for Hodder and Stoughton Educational, a division of
Hodder and Stoughton Ltd, Mill Road, Dunton Green,
Sevenoaks, Kent.

Copyright © 1985 Michael Carrier and Simon Haines.
ISBN 0 340 33400 2